WORDS IN COLOUR IN THE CLASSROOM

To Perceive and to Write

Sister Mary Leonore Murphy, R.S.C.

EDUCATIONAL EXPLORERS
READING . BERKSHIRE . ENGLAND

First published in Great Britain 1970
by Educational Explorers Limited
40 Silver Street, Reading RG1 2SU
© Sister Mary Leonore Murphy, R.S.C., 1970
SBN 85225 536 5

Cover illustration by Gareth Floyd

Printed in Great Britain
by Lamport Gilbert Printers Ltd
Reading, Berkshire.
Set in Monotype Times Roman

TO PERCEIVE AND TO WRITE

CONTENTS

ILLUSTRATIONS

I OFFER MY GRATITUDE

to the Grade 2 children of St Francis' School, Paddington, New South Wales, Australia, for working with me to complete this book,

to Mother M. St Margaret R.S.C., Sister M. Eulalia R.S.C. and Sister M. Aquinas R.S.C., for their proof-reading and constructive criticism,

and to Margaret Greenham and Gwen Oldfield for typing the script.

My sincere thanks are again due to the Department of Medical Illustration, St Vincents Hospital, Sydney, for the photographic studies illustrating this volume.

S. M. LEONORE MURPHY R.S.C.

Sydney, N.S.W., Australia

Foreword

SISTER LEONORE has a fertile mind, and because she has made herself sensitive to children's creative powers could produce extensive educational documents every year. But in addition to this faculty of appreciation Sister Leonore possesses an original turn of mind and has much to teach all educators.

When this book was finished two years ago it was, in the writer's view, a continuation of her first book on Creative Writing, but to my mind it was much more. It ought to be looked at for what it brings in fact rather than what a writer (who enjoys the gift of modesty) believed it brought—I found that it deserved a more important presentation and called it 'To Perceive and to Write'. Sister Leonore agreed to the title when she understood what I, as the first reader, discerned in her story.

It struck me that here was a teacher who had understood that we neither talk nor write unless we have something to say, and recognised that the first duty of a teacher is to provide experiences which inspire the desire to express what one goes through.

Teachers of my generation will know that the preacher-educators of the nineteen-twenties believed that one educated oneself by studying the environment and much was written then of 'centres of interest', 'study of the neighbourhood', on visits to factories, sites, museums, etc. In this book a new dimension is added by Sister Leonore and I was moved to sum it up in the word 'Perceive'. In contrast to the New Education Fellowship stress on knowledge gained through the study of the subjects as they were found immersed in the social and natural environments, Sister Leonore offers a variety of experiences in the rich world of nature and society, as means to become more sensitive, hence to increase one's chances of growing in relationship to one's habitat.

Writing is not an end in itself. Though at school we believed we had to work specifically on the technical aspects of writing, what is

7

attempted here is to 'charge' children with affective and intellectual experiences which sort themselves out, and gain their significance, when objectified under the pen on paper.

Sister Leonore knows that each of her pupils is a person and is in many and various ways endowed. So, she does not stop at writings she gives each person a spectrum of opportunities to receive impact; and of expressing what they believe they lived through. She gathers for us a selection from an enormous field. Much more has been produced in her classes than can be presented between the covers of a book, but we felt less sad at having to be selective when we realised that every teacher inspired by Sister Leonore's work will fill walls and tables with what his or her students will generate. According to the skill and the circumstances of those involved, the yield will differ qualitatively and quantitatively from what we present here. Our task as publishers is to put into circulation texts that will serve our readers rather than discourage them when they meet what could be the final answer to any question.

In so far as I could perceive what the message of this book is, I have been able to write these words.

C. GATTEGNO
General Editor

1
Kaleidoscope

OUR WORDS IN COLOUR JOURNEY is over and we
have in very fact arrived. Disembarking happily, groups of excited
children are savouring the delightful fruits of using the whole Fidel,
and of being able to write any English word they may need in their
creative writing. This is the climax of the course, the reward of
earlier endeavours. Yet it is also a stage that needs to be carefully
handled because there is no longer any restriction of signs. The free
use of English, which the child has just acquired, needs tactful
supervision so that his formulating judgement may become sound
and reliable. Since arriving is not living, and disembarking is not
dwelling, the young child will be at home in his use of written
English only if ample opportunities are provided for creative
writing on topics that are stimulating and intensely interesting to
him. His former gains need to be well established in this, the final
stage of Words in Colour: Stage 4.

With the full kaleidoscope of the Words in Colour signs at his
disposal, the child may turn and re-turn it to create meaningful
patterns of English that are as varied as they are colourful. While
Words in Colour is the medium for the learner's artistry, this
medium has transformed and refined not the work of art but the
young artist himself. By its means the powers of the child's mind
have been educated and his dynamic imagery exercised in trans-
forming, restoring, and uniting images in order that he may generate
new and creative forms.

It is not surprising, then, as we look around at the groups of
children who have completed the Words in Colour programme, to
note how much they have gained over and above the ability to read.
It is evident that Dr Gattegno is right in affirming that reading
may be viewed as a by-product of this scheme. These children
show a poise and confidence that is born of taking the responsibility
for their own learning, making their own decisions, and using their
ingenuity and initiative to write meaningfully with a limited but

gradually expanding vocabulary. Words in Colour has provided them with intellectual rather than rote learning and their work has been individually originated rather than teacher-dominated. Thus they have experienced the elation of personal success at every stage of the journey and radiate the serene gladness that crowns creative achievement.

A Grade 2 class is capable of completing the first three stages of the Words in Colour course in one school term or even less. Then will follow Stage 4, which comprises not only an extension of the art of creative writing, but also vocabulary enrichment, spelling skills, English grammar, and expression. This stage includes the continuous use of the reading ability now acquired, appreciation of prose and poetry, the use of library books, magazines, reference books, and individual learning materials such as the S.R.A. Reading Laboratories,[1] the R.F.U. Laboratory[2] or the E.D.L. Programmes,[3] etc. Linguistics and a study of the English language will have their place in an English course that extends through the Primary and into the Secondary school.

Verse-making will be fostered even in the Infant school. It may emerge as a natural outcome of the environment and stimulus the teacher has provided. Certain it is that creative writing cannot be taught but must be released and guided.

Once the mechanics of Words in Colour are understood, the kernel of the hard phonic nut is revealed. Children then speed on to Stage 4 and enter the realm of free creative writing where the keenness and spontaneity of the class proclaim that writing is exciting.

How is spelling handled?
How can a favourable atmosphere for free creative writing be produced?
What topics do seven-year-olds enjoy?
Can Infant school children write verse?

In this account of some of the activities of a Grade 2 class during one school year, I have attempted to answer these questions.

Come with me into a classroom bright with children's artwork

[1] Science Research Associates Reading Laboratory comprises sets of reading cards which give a multilevel developmental basic programme in comprehension and rate of reading.

[2] Reading for Understanding produced by the Science Research Associates, is a laboratory of graded cards which exercise the pupil in understanding, judging, and evaluating what has been read.
Educational Developmental **Laboratories (McGraw-Hill, New York)** includes controlled reading programmes on special filmstrips which are designed to build up in the pupil the comprehension skills of recall, association, interpretation, and evaluation, as well as an increase in his rate of reading.

and occupied by an enthusiastic group of seven-year-olds who have proved to me that for more than two decades I have under-estimated the potential of children. They have shown me that Words in Colour develops their ability to work at a higher intellectual level than I had ever believed possible. In proof of this, their creative work is as full of colourful surprises as a kaleidoscope. It is as balanced, too, and as perfectly proportioned, as uniquely individual, and quite as fascinating.

2

Words for our work

Spelling with Words in Colour—Stages 1, 2, 3

IN 'CREATIVE WRITING' I have described how we
gathered words from each table of signs to use for our creative
writing. Spelling plays an important part in this writing and is
considered by many teachers to be a major problem. With Words in
Colour, however, spelling presents no difficulty. In the first three
stages letter names are not used, but children link signs to form
words.

How can the child select the correct signs for a word when he has
more than a score from which to choose?

How can he spell so easily and so effortlessly?

To my mind the answer to these questions lies in the correct
use of all the activities of Words in Colour, because they combine
to give the child the ability to read and write English effectively.
Perhaps the most important factor of all is the use of the restricted
field of signs, because the techniques of Words in Colour establish
the child in the facile and discriminate use of these signs. The
word charts are indispensable as the means by which signs are
introduced in the context of words. These words are immediately
made meaningful in sentences by the use of Visual Dictation 2.
The Work Sheet exercises include extension of charted vocabulary.
Experience shows that the best results are obtained if children offer
their additional words for general discussion so that the class may
judge the correctness of the suggestions and share ideas. The
teacher stands by to assess the response, and to raise the standard
if necessary. Thus the child's judgement is educated so that when
challenged for the correct form of a word he will select the right
signs, even if there be more than a score from which to choose.

There are other factors which contribute to the child's spelling
ability: throughout the Words in Colour course, lists of words are
built up, written, and illustrated. These words are used in the

composition of sentences or creative writing. Gradually, a series of spelling 'rules' is discovered spontaneously and learnt by continuous use. The rule is never stated, but the child is quite sure in his application of it, as also in his knowledge of exceptions. I shall give a few examples:

Before the final *y* as in funny, daddy, etc., the second sign in the column of consonants in the World Building Book or Fidel, consisting of double letters, is used.

After a short vowel the *ck* is invariable in such words as sick, trick, truck, lock, etc., but after a long vowel the third consonant sign with the silent *e* is used in like, take, broke, etc. The absorption of the silent *e* into the preceding colour preserves left-to-right eye movement and prevents any unwieldy treatment of this final *e*.

The *er* in butter, pepper, ladder, or summer is usually preceded by the second consonant sign. This comes very easily to the child and he puts the known words *but*, *pep*, *lad*, and *sum* to new and more interesting use. Some exceptions, such as winter and liner will be suggested, discussed, and known in a few moments.

Signs with many sounds are introduced simultaneously, so that the child may use analogies and contrasts to help him to formulate his associations and build up his inner criteria. For example *oe* is to be found in toe, does, shoes, and amoeba. Thus he has an expanding picture of English and is empowered to make his own decisions. Errors on the child's part indicate to the teacher the direction her work should take, unless the mistake was a pure slip, in which case the child can easily set it right unaided. Since, then, the medium is consistent and the method cumulative, spelling techniques develop rapidly and are used with great assurance.

At all times Words in Colour emphasises the importance of perception in its spelling techniques. The child has a visual image of a word and uses his auditory sense in hearing it, his kinaesthetic sense in feeling it in lip-throat-hand alliance, and he cements the visual impression by writing it. To this I add the feel of the synthesis of signs into words in the use of Visual Dictation 1.

Since the manner of word recall differs in each person, flexible methods are essential in order to allow each child to form his associations in a way best suited to himself. Rigid methods of spelling depend on a monotonous repetition of letter names; they fail the child because memory is so inconstant. By contrast, Words in Colour is flexible enough to accommodate any child, be his mode of perception visual, auditory, or kinaesthetic, or should his word recall be made from his mental image. Furthermore, Words in Colour, by its exercises in completions and transformations and by its analytic and synthetic techniques, strengthens the child's power to formulate mental images.

In one experimental year my Grade 2 completed their study of Words in Colour to the end of Stage 3 in the first term. We then began Stage 4 with a detailed study of the Fidel.

In the vertical extension exercise, children suggested words for each sign in a given colour-column. For example, I indicated the first sign *oo* in the light-fawn column and asked, 'Would there be many or few words with this sign'? Children answered that there would be many. They then contributed words or wrote a personal list: kookaburra, woodpecker, footpath, etc. The sign *ou* was then studied. Children remarked that there were only a few of these: should, could, would, and their derivatives. The next sign, *u*, was a popular one, and children were ready with their words: butcher bush, platypus, push, bullet, pudding, etc. The last sign *o* would give only woman and wolf, so 'very few' was the estimation.

This exercise shows how familiar a class can be with the Fidel. I never cease to be amazed at the keenly discriminate listening power with which children are endowed.

Another interesting Fidel study is that of comparing words formed with identical signs in different colour-columns. For example *oo* as in blood is yellow; in moon it is leaf-green; in book it is fawn; in brooch it is light brown. This is also an exercise in aural discrimination and establishes a previously realised fact that if the colour is different the sound will be different. In addition it gives children ready use of the range of sounds over which they exercise their judgement when confronted, in black-and-white print, with a sign applying to several sounds. At first their minds make a deliberate choice; later, in the fluent reading of Stage 4, this process is instantaneous. With some proper nouns, such as the names of places and people, a trial-and-error session may be heard, as children experiment with the possibilities, to discover the right pronunciation. This gradually becomes for them a spontaneous exercise and finally, in Stage 4, they are equal to reading and writing any proper noun put before them. For example, my Grade 2 enjoyed the challenge of such words as Antarctica, hydro-electric scheme, Mt Kosciusko, etc.

In Stage 4 we introduce alphabet letter-names. These are familiar to the children and so the transition from signs to letter-names and back is effected in a matter of minutes. We made the extraordinary and exciting discovery that the Words in Colour child can spell just as easily with letter-names as with the signs, and that he can visualise the component parts of a word and in so doing, can spell far more effectively than his older brothers and sisters, who rely on their memory.

14

Our first spelling game is a simple one. I choose a sign from a word-family that will give a prolific response e.g., *oi*. The rule for this game is that any word employing these two letters may be spelt, irrespective of its sound. Children prove that the gap between Words in Colour and traditional spelling with letter-names is now bridged effortlessly. They spell rapidly and accurately, often closing their eyes in order to visualise clearly the particular progression of sounds. As each word is spelt, I write it on the chalkboard. Should an error be made I notice that the class is aware immediately. I recommend the child to *say* the word. This is usually enough to unravel the tangle, because the feel of the word in syllabification elucidates the correct progression of signs and hence the spelling. Sometimes, for the visual-image child, I find it necessary to write his incorrect form on the chalkboard. He often rectifies his mistake at once. If not, discussion ensues, the word is decoded and encoded by class members, and finally by the child who made the initial error. When given the letters *oi*, children volunteered the following words and spelt them correctly: oil, coil, spoil, point, Potts Point, Darling Point, viewpoint, noise, noisy, coinage, poison, poisonous, etc.

With *ou* children devised: would, house, touch, cough, thorough, pouch, through, though, ground, plough, should, out, soul, bough, pounds, doubt, mountain, playground, hour, could, rough, outside, mouse, etc. The letters *or* evoked the following response: work, horse, world, shore, corn, sailor, horror, workman, born, tailor, silkworm, Lord, for, fort, more, morning star, fork, etc. At the close of this exercise, which amounts to a matter of minutes, the board is full of interesting words. For this reason we call this game 'Fill the Board'.

Thematic word game

Our second game is thematic, in that it centres around a certain topic. The general round of lessons in the Infant school affords rich and varied themes, e.g., Religious Knowledge, Social Studies, Natural Science, Picture Study, Poetry Reading, Poetry Appreciation, Stories, Music, Art, Health, and Safety. Our school television programmes are useful for this game. Children enjoy note-taking during the session and then gather to contribute words for general discussion.

After Term 1 they spell out their words using letter-names and I record on the chalkboard exactly what they say. After a session on the theme 'vineyards' the list read: vineyard, dip-tins, drying-racks, frost-alarm, farm, grapes, drying, chemical, Sunraysia, bunch, leaves, stems, etc.

15

After 'housing' children contributed: building, foundation, concrete, reservoir, electrician, plumber, floor-boards, tiles, etc. The word 'moddun' was given, but when I recorded it a general dissent arose. The child corrected his error, found the component signs on the Fidel, and wrote the word 'modern'. Thenceforth all children knew it. There was no need to repeat and repeat it.

Other lists included:

Soft-bodied animals: shell, mollusc, mantle, head, chiton, bubble shell, octopus, oyster, clam shell, invertebrates.

Cold-blooded animals: amphibians, toad, frog, newt, reptiles, lizards, snakes, blue-tongued lizard, goannas, tortoise. The latter was given as 'tortose' but was corrected by the child, found on the Fidel, and written. It was known by the entire class when tested later.

Jointed-legged animals: suit, armour, greyfish, insect, head, cicada, bee, butterfly, eyes, ants, crustacea, thorax. This word was spelt 'thorace' but was spontaneously rectified by the same child as soon as he had complied with my suggestion to say the word.

Warm-blooded animals: swan, flipper, webbed, bower bird, lyre bird, pee-wee, eagle, swimming, seagull, hooked beak, quills, ibis, penguins.

Looking over children's lists I found that the word 'penguin' was incorrectly spelt by a few children. I wrote the word on the chalk-board and we discussed it. The light aqua sign *u* was identified, the word found on the Fidel and written with ease. There has been no difficulty in spelling it since then.

Making a calendar: calendar, date, night, summer, moon, sun-rise, lunar day, hours, minutes, autumn, leap year, waxing, waning, year, column, daylight, earth, telescope, rotation.

Natural Science

Another fertile soil for word-cultivation is to be found in the direct observation of living things. One day in September I took a snail to school. As the children gathered around to watch it, a spontaneous and interesting discussion developed which resulted in the following vocabulary: snail, shell, inside-out, crawling, slowly, foot, slide, slime, silvery, trail, feelers, horn, eyes, touch, sensitive, pest, slippery, protection, etc.

It will be noted that these words are more descriptive than the factual lists gleaned from the television lessons. No doubt this was caused by the intense interest of the children in the living creature and by the general discussion and questioning which set them searching their minds for the appropriate vocabulary. Yet, though I worked for a release of apt words, I found that the majority of the children had but a limited store. I realised how important it is for the teacher to add to their word-power by contributing personally, in the best English style, using words more tellingly descriptive than those of which they yet have command.

This is the moment for the reading of an appropriate poem or story to lift the children's ideas and set them thinking. The poem or story may be deemed of high quality if it can do just that—leave children wondering, not quite satisfied, because everything has not been said; leave them full of thought-provoking questions which their own minds can solve for them; leave them, finally, reaching out for conclusions at which they can arrive by means of their intellect.

Stories

Stories can be used as an impetus to vocabulary enrichment. Many examples come to my mind, but I mention one that my seven-year-olds really enjoyed. It happened in October that, a few days after we had entertained visitors at school, a large flat parcel arrived in our classroom. I opened it in the sight of all and a bright picture book was revealed, bearing the title *The Lion and the Rat*. Books are made to be savoured, not set aside, and this was meant for *us*. Children were never so ready for a story as they were for that surprise-packet illustrated by Brian Wildsmith. They gathered in a close group to feast their eyes on the gay, almost unique, illustrations. The story, from La Fontaine, was told with utmost simplicity, but it was the illustrations that embroidered the tale. After the first appraisal we used the text for a language exercise. The meaning was discussed. Then children's vocabulary was extended in the finding of descriptive words for the actions and feelings of the animal characters; for example, words describing

the rat: quiet, hairy, frightened, clever, thoughtful, cunning;

the lion: majestic, proud, strong, shaggy;

the forest: mysterious, creepy, forbidding, 'scary', gloomy, deep;

the captured lion: shrieking, screaming, snarling, fighting, angry, in a temper, yelling, mad (some of his yells and threats were translated);

the animals: rushing, bounding, galloping, prancing, racing, hurrying; curious;

the animals encountering the lion: helpless, anxious, worried, afraid, disappointed in their King, fearful (this picture was marvellously expressive—each animal-face reflected his own particular emotions);

the abandoned lion: deserted, lonely, rejected, let-down;

the helpful rat of the final episode: thoughtful, unselfish, brave, a quiet worker, brainy, clever, grateful, keeping his word, making the most of what he had.

17

My comments at this stage rounded off their ideas and introduced a new word: 'I think the little rat was very resourceful, don't you? That was what Marianne meant when she said he was making the most of what he had.'

Most stories require no analysis and are used in the Infant school for appreciation of the beauty of their language and for sheer enjoyment. The English style of the well-chosen story unconsciously influences children's choice of words and their speech patterns. Beatrix Potter's works are such, and *Donkey's Glory* by Nan Goodall. Some suitable Fairy Tales from Anderson and Grimm should be included, and a selection made from the folk stories so delightfully told by either Elizabeth Clarke or Berta Lawrence. These are but a few examples of the wealth of delightful literature for young children.

Biblical parables have their place in the Infant school. I like to prepare for these by relating some simple allegorical story, e.g., *Raggy*, from the works of M. de la Cruz. Once the idea of discovering the meaning underlying the 'Puzzle Story' is grasped, children are ready to draw inferences hidden between the lines of the parables.

The exercises of Words in Colour have paved the way for this new type of transformation which is an intellectual substitution of something that has a likeness to what has been metaphorically named. The understanding of signs and symbols is an important part of daily living. Babies in their cradles interpret the moods, feelings, and attitudes of their environment when these are communicated to them through the tones and overtones of voices around them, or the expressions of faces, or even the less communicable atmosphere surrounding them. As growing children they infer a root cause from an experienced effect and govern their actions by it: 'Pussy has wire in his feet' said one scratched toddler, and he avoided pulling the 'wiry' animal's tail again.

The gospel stories of the life of Our Lord are of exceptional importance in the education of the young child. They provide him with a spiritual and intellectual experience and give him the opportunity to use language that will convey his personal and prayerful thought. In this way the subjective rather than the objective approach of earlier themes is accentuated.

My example concerns an experience with a gospel discussion in Grade 2 in October. I chose the story of the Cure of the Blind Man and told it simply, without the use of pictures, because children had recently seen the film *The Greatest Story Ever Told* and had images of the scene. We thought about blindness and tried to realise what the other senses would mean to a person deprived of sight. This was a true application of the senses, for touch, taste, hearing, and smell

18

were each considered. I had on hand some sweet-smelling citrus blossoms and lemon-scented leaves. Children inhaled the cloying sweetness of the blossoms, and crushed the leaves to breathe the crisp lemon scent. The free creative writing that resulted will be found in Chapter 8 and is worth perusing.

Another fruitful area for vocabulary extension is picture study. One wintry day in July, I pinned up a beautiful *Child Education* picture which typified the season. Picture study for us usually means making a journey, a journey into the picture. We look at the beauty around us, listen to the conversation of the people and the sounds of nature, smell the aromas we imagine would be there, touch some of the things we see, think of what happened before and what will happen after the scene that is depicted. Then we may wish anything we like about the people or the happenings or ourselves. Sometimes we learn a lesson from the picture or decide about something we would like to do.

Empathy is a strong characteristic in children, so we may think also of how the people feel, or how we should feel if we were there. There is no rigidity about following all these avenues of thought. The whole lesson is refreshing and children often ask for another trip to such a place.

In this study of the winter scene, descriptive sentences were composed orally and many meaningful words suggested which would appear at a later date in children's writing:

frosty, sparkling, tingling, protected, bare, arching, slippery, pattering, waterproof, excited, chirping, cheeping, pecking, twittering, evergreens, berries.

Musical appreciation

The musical appreciation lesson provides a new world of listening experiences for the child. It soon becomes evident, however, that music cannot be studied in isolation, because the arts are so inter-related. Great paintings, works of literature, and musical compositions have many features in common. In each there is to be found a rhythmic form, an intrinsic movement, a mood, a colour or tone and a structural proportion and balance. In examining the mood of a selection, the child may try to discover the ideas in the composer's mind, or he may build his own story to suit his personal interpretation of the music.

It is the task of the teacher to develop a keen awareness of these characteristics in her young charges so that they may become

19

sensitive to the best in music and know how to appreciate it. From this awareness will flow many kinds of expression-work in either physical response or in words that are spoken or written. It is in proportion to the deepening and widening of a child's experience that his vocabulary will be expanded. The teacher will therefore take care not to over-simplify her language but will deliberately use correct musical terms, remembering also that there are no adequate synonyms available. Words such as *allegro, ritardando, crescendo, piano, forte, legato, staccato, overture, suite,* etc., as well as the names of the instruments and the composers, can be managed quite easily by seven-year-olds and should be used by the teacher at the appropriate times.

In studying a musical extract, children should reflect on how it makes them *feel*: sad, happy, contented, peaceful, frightened, anxious, etc. They may offer appropriate titles to fit in with their ideas before the teacher tells them the composer's title for the piece. Thus they may say: 'A Spring Morning', 'Boating on the Lake', 'The Storm', 'The Picnic'. They may be asked to describe the sound of certain instruments; e.g., loud, heavy, ponderous, dainty, staccato, or they may be encouraged to liken the sound to something they are familiar with: 'It's like raindrops on the roof'; 'It sounds like a train rushing by'.

Children should also be led to contrast new musical extracts with known ones. Thus a Grade 2 child was heard to say: '*Petite Ballerina* is dainty and light, but *Bydlo* is lumbering and heavy'.

Above all, the teacher should ensure that the musical appreciation lesson is an enjoyable experience and for that reason she will avoid labouring the verbalisations on the part of the children. After the initial listening time, the first reaction may well be physical response to the music. This will be done by appropriate body movements, which may be flowing or jerky, heavy or light, quick, slow or gradual, according to the rhythm, tempo, and dynamics of the extract. Creative writing or art-expression may follow later. The teacher will judge when the time is ripe for vocabulary enrichment or creative writing.

It may happen that the visual impact of a dancer seen on film interpreting a ballet may trigger spontaneous writing as nothing else could. Examples of a whole class response to the viewing of *Giselle* are included in Chapter 7. On that occasion, before the children commenced writing, they compiled a thematic word list containing such words as: *ballet, point-shoes, movement, dance, twisting, twirling, graceful, glide, dainty, partner, Giselle, Prince,* etc. In this way, if they possess a suitable vocabulary of words they are prompted to use, children will write with more sincerity and confidence and with natural rhythmic grace and charm.

It has been said that of all the Arts the most contagious is Poetry. The child who listens to, loves, and lives with poetry will break easily and almost spontaneously into rhythmic expression when strong emotions urge him to write. That is why Words in Colour is so important in the Infant school. It is the means whereby the child is able to express himself in free creative writing when his exuberance and enthusiasm are at their height. Only strong feelings can be crystallised into jewel-like prose or poured out in the flowing cadences of singing words. Such feelings depend upon personal experience and upon the education of the child's awareness.

The importance of the reading of poetry in every class of the Infant school cannot be too strongly emphasised. By its means the intellectual powers of the child are more fully developed, his emotions trained, his judgements formed, and the world of his imagination enlarged. Furthermore, good literature, be it poetry or prose, provides him with a healthy emotional outlet.

Poetry reading may occur incidentally during the Infant school day to suit a mood or an experience. At times only a few lines may be needed to convey the meaning. For example:

> Can you dance?
> I love to dance!
> Music is my happy chance . . .
> > E. FARJEON

> The world is very old
> But year by year
> It groweth young again
> When buds appear . . .
> > C. M. BARKER

> The sea is a hungry dog
> Giant and grey . . .
> > JAMES REEVES

> Here's Spring
> With green on his wing . . .
> > E. FARJEON

> 'Son,'
> My father used to say,
> 'Don't run'. . . .
> 'Words',
> My father used to say,
> 'Scare birds.' . . .
> > D. McCORD

21

There will, of course, be longer lessons to provide time for the enjoyment and appreciation of the full text of the above poems and others, as well as for dramatising poems, for experimenting with dialogue, movement, or with choral speaking. It is advisable, however, to teach by heart only those poems that the class really enjoys. It should be the children's prerogative to decide whether they like a poem enough to live with it. Such favourites abound in the works of A. A. Milne, R. L. Stevenson, Eleanor Farjeon and others. Sometimes it is profitable to interest the children in the poet as a person and let them study a group of poems by the one author. For this purpose I make available to my Grade 2 copies of such books as *When We Were Very Young* and *Now We are Six* by A. A. Milne, and *A Child's Garden of Verses* by R. L. Stevenson. Children so enjoy this personal appraisal of poetry in its printed form that these books are the most popular in the class library.

When poems are chosen for appreciation it is well to include the delightfully refreshing works of Christina Rossetti and Rose Fyleman in order to share with children the fresh rhythmic patterns and word-pictures that are exceptionally beautiful. Anthologies of poetry for children are abundant and most useful. I think May Hill Arbuthnot in her work *Time For Poetry* has, in the variety and quality of her selection, compiled one of the best of these. Paperback volumes, *Four Feet and Two* (Leila Berg) and *A Puffin Quartet of Poets*, hold treasures for children. The Australian production, *One Sunday Morning Early* by Irene Gough is a real gem, bright with humour and sparkling gaiety and full of authentically vivid imagery of the Australian scene. Ffrida Wolfe, E. Maddox Roberts and Walter de la Mare have each a wealth of beauty for our children. Of his contribution Walter de la Mare says, 'Only the rarest kind of best can be good enough for the young'.

Given the best in all its rarity, with the most stimulating environment to provide a balanced development for each individual in our care, we notice our children growing mentally more aware and more mature. We see them accepting the responsibility for their own learning, solving their problems thoughtfully, and manifesting an originality of ideas that is, at times, quite startling. This revelation of the child's inner personality is never more evident than in free creative writing, examples of which abound in this book. This writing is the outcome of our day-to-day living in school, where we find ourselves measuring up to Pestalozzi's yardstick, 'It is life which educates'.

So we amass words for our work of writing. The adventure of so doing is exhilarating and absorbing. Children gradually become word conscious. Indeed many of them have, at their own request, received dictionaries instead of other gifts on their special days.

Word-power is a mighty weapon for young children to acquire. Even in underprivileged areas it can be given to them if the teacher turns every opportunity to good account.

The only path for a child to follow in order to achieve good quality in creative writing lies along the way of experimentation and practice. As true art cannot be forced or copied and depends upon the expression of intense personal experience, so too the free creative writing of Stage 4 is but dry bones unless there is breathed into it the excitement of writing, the urge to express personal thoughts and feelings, and the longing to play with words until they say just what the child wishes to express.

The Card Game described in *Creative Writing* has already been of inestimable value in giving the class an appreciation of the function of words and the ability to manipulate them to convey shades of meaning or to alter the context. Hence our children already write with great variety in sentence structure.

We must go further, however, and provide a classroom where rhythmic expression, or verse making, is as natural as prose and where children are free to experiment and make their own discoveries about the behaviour of rhythmic word-patterns. Coined words are not frowned upon, because they express a personal urge to convey a shade of meaning for which the child lacks a suitable word. So when Raymond wrote of the snail 'Here comes a slippery slimer', I marvelled at his ingenuity.

Word lists as such are useless. They are idle bricks and stones. They need to be built up into a construction of elegance, or one of solid beauty, or a fairy-tale palace not made with hands. Nothing equals creativity in developing a child's personality. It is the expression of his being, the opening of small shutters where momentarily he reveals his soul. To write thus, he must feel at ease and be full of peaceful confidence in those who are to share his inmost thoughts. As in his art work the seven-year-old is less inhibited than his ten-year-old brother or sister, so in free creative writing he is delightfully natural, candid, confident, and open-hearted.

It is, then, the ideal time to establish this taste for the writing of both verse and prose and to encourage the child in his endeavours. The accelerated pace of Words in Colour gives the young child, as a great gift, this opportunity of working with words. By means of this method he reads fluently at an earlier age and spells and writes creatively sooner than he would by traditional methods. Time is available then for free creative writing to be enjoyed by the Infant school child. On this foundation he should continue to build with gradually increasing awareness throughout his school days.

3

Blue Fanny

You float on air
and softly too!
GLEN, 7

ON THE FIRST DAY OF APRIL, as I opened my class-
room door, I sensed that something was moving; yet, as I glanced
around everything seemed in place. Then I saw it! A beautiful
creature unfolded its wings of iridescent blue edged with black, then
delicately lifted and joined them, like palms of praying hands, to
reveal a paler underside enlivened by touches of crimson. I watched,
fascinated, as I tiptoed nearer to the large glass observation tank.
This has been the home of our Blue Fanny through all the stages of
its existence and now, having burst its pupa-case, it was stretching
its wings. Here in our own classroom was a miracle indeed.

I thought back to the day early in February, when the pearly
egg had been found on our camphor-laurel tree. No, it was not on
the tree itself but on a small sucker-shoot, a red-brown tip that
would remain fresh and tender to nourish the tiny larva. I remem-
bered the interest, especially among my Grade 2 boys, in the changing colour of that egg. With eye to the magnifying glass Glen was
certain that he could see a little black thing move in the egg. He was
right! Soon a minute black caterpillar emerged and was feeding on
the leaf. As the days passed the tiny creature grew, splitting his
skin to become a beautiful olive-green colour. Children took turns
in providing fresh leaf-tips and in cleaning out the tank. Someone
noticed that the head of the caterpillar was growing large and
squarish, giving his whole body a rather triangular shape, and it was
discovered that Blue Triangle is another name for the Blue Fanny.
At this stage a bright lime-yellow band appeared across the head,
sprouting tiny limp feelers at each end, and the strong tail clasper
became a decided blue. We realised the great protection afforded by
camouflage when each morning we had extreme difficulty in locating

our green pet. And then, just before the larva was fully grown, we discovered by accident that it had another defence. I think Antony must have made a sharp pull at it to place it on fresh food, for the caterpillar reacted as to an enemy. We were amazed to see two quarter-inch 'spikes' protrude above the 'nose'. An acrid smell filled the air, and some of the surplus fluid settled on the surprised Antony's hand. It was far from pleasant. As for our caterpillar, he had become quite wrinkled and wizened as if the great effort had been too much for him, and we thought he was going to die. However, once we went back to our work, the fresh leaves interested him and he revived. We agreed not to handle him again but to let him find his own way about. Soon he appeared to be fully grown and we watched carefully for changes. Quite often now he 'silked' a mature green leaf with a thin coating of fine threads and settled there. He was no longer so hungry. What was happening?

It was Antony who first saw the girdle—a silken cord fastened to the leaf and passed right around his body, holding him as if in a sling. None of us saw the caterpillar cast his skin to become a pupa, but there was the wrinkled skin gathered up and thrown off. Now we had a beautiful green leaf-veined creature, no longer interested in food but hanging supported by his silken sling with his one pointed horn held quite erect. He was sleeping. We knew he was alive for occasionally he gave a twitch or a wriggle, and soon the colour and shape of the wings could be seen through the thin pupa walls. Today, at last, the cycle was complete and the pupa shell hung empty. The perfectly formed Blue Fanny had emerged.

This day stands out as the culmination of an experience and the fruition of a long and painstaking study. Imagine the children, drawn to observe, speechless with wonder, fascinated and amazed, whispering to each other yet scarcely daring to breathe, tip-toeing about, running to impart the news, spurred spontaneously to write or draw, and excited with an exultant and pure joy.

Here is Glen, a real boy, sometimes 'tough', who exclaims in tones of emotion I cannot portray with words, 'But . . . it's . . . beautiful!'

It is upon such experiences that creative writing depends. No manner of detailed class lessons on composition can ever bring about that spontaneous appeal to the emotions, that depth of thought, that realisation of the inner meaning of things, as can an observation of such a miracle of nature. The final stage of Words in Colour brings with it this ability for free creative writing by means of which the child may give utterance to his deepest thoughts. So in our classroom the emergence of our Blue Fanny on 1 April set pencils flying as the children expressed themselves thus:

Butterfly

A caterpillar slept for a long time.
Today he came into a butterfly.
He has shiny wings.
The children like him.

PATRICIA, 7

The butterfly can fly so high.
It can float,
It can fly over the trees.
The butterfly goes up and down.

MICHAEL LE. 7

Today the butterfly's pupa split open.
His wings stretched.
He was white and brown and red.
He had six legs.
He was an insect.
He came out on the first of April.
He was small.
First he was a caterpillar,
then came the pupa, and then the butterfly.

LESLIE, 6

On April 1st when I went to school
I saw a butterfly.
It stretched its wings.
It had blue wings with brown, yellow
and red underneath.
It nad six legs.
It was an insect.

CLAUDIO, 7

Today our pupa split his skin off and
turned into a butterfly.
He has bright wings.
He was trying to spread his wings out.
He is so beautiful.
You must be very gentle with him.

MARIANNE, 7

(This little girl has a flair for creative writing. Notice the development through the year of her use of apt expressions and her awareness of rhythm and rhythmic words.)

26

O butterfly how good you are!
You fly so high!
You float on air and softly too.
You fly so lightly
that you're like a feather.

GLEN, 7

O butterfly you flutter in the sky.
You are soft and you have many colours on you.
You are very soft and you fly up and down.
and you glide in the sky.
You float softly.
The wind will push you so that you can fly
a little higher in the sky.

MICHAEL L., 6

(Already this little boy shows keen observation and appreciation of natural beauty.)

4

A treasure-house of knowledge

'. . . old dead things . . .'
MARY, 7

'WE ARE GOING TO THE MUSEUM to look at old dead things', said seven-year-old Mary in disgust to her mother. Mary had not been to our Australian Museum before and did not know what thrilling adventures we had in that treasure-house of knowledge. She had not met our education officer, a popular and gifted teacher, who could lecture with equal ease on any topic in the museum's tremendous coverage of Natural Science and Social Studies, to audiences from Infant level through Secondary school. This was versatility indeed and the children all loved her and her two capable assistants.

I watched Mary's attitude gradually change from the moment our special bus drew up at the museum and things began to happen. We were greeted in the foyer by our education officer and led into the well-equipped lecture hall. An interesting array of insect specimens was laid out in classified groups on the lecturer's desk. These, together with a number of carefully selected colour-slides, the showing of an interesting and appropriate film, and a visit to the gallery to inspect the showcases, served to extend the horizons of the lecture. The abundance and variety of interesting aids, and the expert handling of them, soon clothed the 'old dead things' with the vital spark of scientific study. Mary was fascinated as lifeless forms took on a new meaning and the infinitesimal detail of the perfection of the tiniest living thing began to open up a new world to her. She eventually became one of the keenest pupils as we followed through the year's programme, beginning with this first visit in March.

Twice in every term I took my Grade 2 children to the museum, having previously arranged the subject-matter with the education officer. For the current year our topics were: After the summer holidays—Australian insects; in autumn—Australian aborigines; in winter—Australian mammals and Antarctica; in spring—Australian birds; in summer (the year's end)—rock pools and the seashore.

For about a fortnight prior to our museum visit, I prepared the topic with the children so that they would profit by the lecture and know what to look for in the specimens available. For a week or two afterwards, while factual details were still fresh and clear, children were given ample time for the use of related arts—especially illustration, design, and creative writing.

During the past ten years I have watched with interest the effect on urban children of these regular planned lessons at the museum. Living in a crowded city area they have had little chance to study and appreciate the beauties of nature. But once the door to the wonders of nature was unlocked they entered whole-heartedly; they were at home and they belonged. They might stop to wonder, stand still to admire, or stoop to examine. We agreed with W. H. Davies that this is a poor life if we '. . . have no time to stand and stare'.

Our planned journey through the museum worked throughout the year to complete and extend the children's own discoveries of Natural Science and of the life-patterns of other races. Gradually children matured and became well-informed, keenly observant, poised and confident to meet the demands of the world around them.

During Education Week, which is held in August each year, we have been delighted to participate in the splendid display of children's work at the museum. All contributions were an outcome of lessons held there. The foyer and many of the gallery show-cases were given over to displaying the books, models, paintings, collections, and charts of children in Infant, Primary, and Secondary schools. Our children's illustrations and designs on the topic of the Australian aborigines were usually featured in this display; and then the education officers, as if the credit did not belong to themselves, awarded prizes for outstanding work.

There was Mary, back among the 'old dead things', with an insatiable desire to know all the 'hows' and 'whys' of living things. She was clutching her prize-book awarded for an Aboriginal bark-design of meticulous detail and precision. She was no longer complaining, but proudly elated to have so enjoyed finding the wonder of the living through the dead.

Leafing through the children's writing on museum topics, I linger on these, my favourites:

TERM 1: AUSTRALIAN INSECTS

The Bees

The bees come in and out of the flowers to take honey and to be busy all day through. I hear you, so you buzz and buzz little bees.

SILVANNA, 7

The Grasshopper

One day I found a grasshopper. It had six legs and two feelers. They are bad for the farmer because they eat the crops when they fly in swarms.

MARK R., 6

My Grasshopper

My grasshopper is green and he can jump high. He is the same shade as the grass.

MICHAEL L., 6

My Bees

My little bees are good. They make lots of honey for me. They go around to every flower to get the nectar for the honey.

MICHAEL LE., 7

Fruits

Did you know that fruit comes from flowers? Fruit comes from blossoms. The bee helps the flower to form the fruit. If we did not have bees we would have no fruit.

RAYMOND, 7

Blossoms

Pretty blossoms on the tree
as pretty as a bumble bee.
Bumble bee, bumble bee,
collect pollen from the blossoms on the tree.

MARIANNE, 7

The Bees

I am a little bee, I have a stinger on the end of my body. When I sting you the stinger comes off and stays in you. The queen bee is different. Her stinger does not come out. It is straight.

TIMOTHY, 6

TERM 1: AUSTRALIAN ABORIGINES

Aborigines' Dance

Clap your hands, turn around,
Clap your hands, jump up high
That's what the aborigines do.

CATHERINE, 7

Fishing Spear

One day I was making a fishing spear. I had to put three sharp sticks for the prongs. When I saw the fish I threw it at him.

HELLIO, 7

Spears

'I am going to make a spear,' said Nimble Jack, 'a very fine spear indeed. Now I shall start to carve it. Here is a fine point of flint', he said. 'Now it is finished. Ah here is my victim. There's the kangaroo I aimed at.'

MARK R., 7

Dilly Bags

Dilly bags, dilly bags,
gather up the dilly bags,
Ai ai yar yar!
The day's work is finished.
We sing akayh while we work.
Oor ar lar ra!
Lar ra lar ra!
Akayh la la wa wa!

KIM, 7

Rainbow Serpent

I can make a rainbow serpent
go round and round,
I really can, I really can,
till it touches the ground.

MARIANNE, 7

Boomerang

Look in the air there's a boomerang
there, there, there,
Where?
There!
Over there in the air.

MARIANNE, 7

A Dilly Bag

O how I wish I could have a little silly dilly bag, the one an aborigine made, not one in a shop. I did ask Mum and Dad, but Dad said 'No-o-o-o'.

THERESE, 7

Shields

Today I will make a shield. I will carve it, then I will put the ochre on with some other earth-colours. Now I will start work. It took one day to make it. It is carved out of wood and covered with red-ochre. Now I can play aborigines with my brother and friends in my garden.

MICHAEL LO., 6

Hunting

My husband is going hunting. He's going to teach my son hunting. My husband said we mustn't forget our boomerangs. My son said 'Oh no, we mustn't forget.' Now we are ready to go hunting.

MARY, 7

Dilly Bags

I'm going to get some food, food, food, for my family and me to eat, eat, eat. I must hurry before my husband comes back from hunting.

MARY, 7

Dilly Bags

I have a dilly bag. It is very brown. I go hunting with it, and I got a fish. I brought it home and said 'Guess what I've got for tea?' I said 'A fish,' so we started to cook it.

JULIANNE, 6

Hunting

I go hunting with my dilly bag and I chase worms. I said 'Hurry up, I've got to get some worms.'

JULIANNE, 6

Rainbow Serpent

If you find some brick and get a brown and white colour and then go round and round and round like a snail's shell, you will have a rainbow serpent.

MARK A., 7

Aborigines

Clap, clap, clap,
We are dancing on our feet.
We are dancing a corroboree.
We say 'Ooo ar ar ar!'
Stamp our feet and turn around
Scream, 'Arrrrr . . .!'

MICHAEL LE., 7

Aborigines Song

Clap your hands and sit down low,
Hear the aborigines play their didgeridoos,
Drum, drum, drum, drum, drum, drum,
I hear the aborigines play.

SHARON, 6

Shields

'Woola, woola, I will make a shield. I will call my mum' said the boy, 'and now I can go hunting with the boys and dad'.

GLEN, 7

▲Mark R. and Maryanne work at S.R.A. or R.F.U. cards while Kim and Catherine consult the keys. The tabulated scores are displayed behind Kim.

▼'The Word Charts are indispensable.' Therese uses Visual Dictation 2 to indicate a sentence.

▼'. . . the intense interest of the children in living creatures . . .' Michael Lo., and Antony are fascinated by the snails.

▲Visual Dictation 1 is used throughout the Words in Colour course for word building and spelling. In Stage 4, a detailed study of the Fidel is made.
▼The card game is of inestimable value for teaching variety in sentence structure.

Shields

I was making a shield and then I painted it and decorated it. Then I tested it by putting it on the ground and throwing spears at it. But it was hard!

ANTON, 7

Shields

I once was making a shield. It had brown colours. It had lots of patterns on it. My shield protects me from any harm.

ANTONY, 7

Aborigines

Aborigines have a corroboree and they do it very well. One day a little boy wanted to be like his father, so he clapped his hands and danced around.

PATRICIA, 7

Aboriginal Song

Clap your hands!
Jump up high!
Play the clappers
And have good fun!
(Let's do it again)
Clap your hands!
Jump up high!
Play the clappers.
And have good fun!

TIMOTHY, 6

(A delightfully rhythmic song with an unusual polka-beat).

TERM 2: AUSTRALIAN MAMMALS

Wombat

Wombat, wombat, what do you eat?
I eat grass and worms,
and I walk on my little feet.

MICHAEL L., 7

Museum

We went to the Museum. We saw the spiny ant-eater and many other animals. I liked the koala and the kangaroo. The most important is the platypus, because it is so wonderful.

GLEN, 7

Kangaroo

I am a kangaroo. I live in the Australian bushland. I eat grass. I hop around on my hind legs and balance on my long tail. I am a Mother kangaroo and I carry my Joey in my pouch.

KIM, 7

33

What am I?

I live in a tree,
I eat leaves and sometimes fruit.
I come out in the night.
Apples are my favourite fruit.
My fur is soft.
Some people trap me.
What am I?
(I am a possum).

MARK R., 7

Kangaroo

I am a kangaroo so great and tall.
This is my little one so great and small.
I feed her on milk, can't you see?
We're as happy as happy as happy can be.

MARIANNE, 7

Wombat

I am a wombat nice and fat.
I make my home in the bush.
I like my home because it's fat too.

MICHAEL L., 7

Mammals

Mammals usually have fur. Some have pouches and some have not. The most famous mammal is the kangaroo.

KIM, 7

Mammals

A mammal has fur. The mother of the little animal feeds it on milk. A kangaroo has a pouch in which to keep the little animal warm.

CARMELLA, 8

(Carmella, a New Australian, had no command of English at all last year.)

Mammals

Mammals are animals that are warm blooded, also they suckle their young. Some have pouches.

MARK R., 7

(Mark R., is a gifted boy who has profited greatly from the extension exercises of Words in Colour. His vocabulary is precise and meaningful.)

34

Flying Fox

Once upon a time I saw a flying fox. He flies high in the sky. He only has fur on his body. He eats fruit. He can hang from the tree. He pulls the fruit branch down with his claws.

MARK A., 7

(Flying Fox represented a great triumph for Mark A., and gave him a taste for writing.)

Bandicoot

I like lovely little bandicoot digging for insects and worms. I woke up yesterday. I went outside and I saw holes in the ground. Then what do you think I saw? A little bandicoot!

RAYMOND, 7

Kangaroo's Baby

One day Mother Kangaroo found that her baby was missing. She looked all over the place and did not find it. So she went to the farmer. Mother Kangaroo said, 'Did you see my baby?' 'Yes, here he is.' 'Thank you,' said Mother Kangaroo.

GRANT, 7

Platypus

I swim in the water.
I have a big big nose.
I feed my babies on milk,
Soon they will grow up.

CARMEN, 7

Possum

I am a ring-tailed possum.
I am called a ring-tailed possum
because I have a ring on my tail.
Sometimes I swing from branch to branch.
I like being a possum because it is fun for me.

TIMOTHY, 6

TERM 2: WILD-LIFE IN ANTARCTICA

Museum

At the Museum I saw a petrel and a whale. I got a prize for the Aboriginal shield I painted for Education Week. My Mother and Father were very proud of me.

ROBERT, 7

About Whales

The biggest whale is the blue whale.
A sperm whale eats squids.
A dolphin looks like a whale.
The factory ship has a hole at one end.
It is a slip way through which the whales are pulled on board.

MICHAEL, L., 7

Whales

Whales are the biggest mammals in the world. The blue whale is the biggest of them all. It has no teeth but it has baleen. The best thing it likes to eat is krill.

CATHERINE, 7

Penguins

Penguins cannot fly but they can swim.
They use their little wings for swimming.
They slide on their tummies on icey hills.

WADE, 7

The Penguins

Penguins can swim very well but they cannot fly. They have flippers to swim with but they have no wings for flying. When they go for a swim they have to make sure that the leopard seal is not there. So they push one of the penguins in and if he does not come back they do not go in.

SHARON, 7

TERM 3: AUSTRALIAN BIRDS

Honeyeaters

A honeyeater sticks its beak into the flower. Then it sucks the nectar off its tongue.

LESLIE, 7

Birds

Birds have wings. They have food of all sorts. They fly around the sky, you see.

CARMEN, 7

Owl

Owl, owl, in the dark night,
you fly and screech all over the town
when everyone is asleep.

MARIANNE, 7

36

Birds

Happily the birds are singing and chirping.
They love the things they eat, and they fly over bushes,
high into the sky.

MICHAEL LE., 7

The Lyre Bird

The lyre bird has many different colours in its feathers and it makes strange noises. It runs through the bushes looking for worms. It has long feathers in its tail.

MICHAEL LE., 7

The Eagle

I hear an eagle squealing
as loud as loud can be.
He swoops down to the ground
to get the rabbits there.

CHRISTINE, 7

Birds

Birds, Birds, smooth and soft,
you fly so swiftly in the sky
and other little birds
spy your nest.

JULIANNE, 7

(At this lecture children were permitted to hold bird specimens and group themselves into bird 'families'. Thus they formed the parrot-family, the bower-bird family, the kingfisher family, etc. The class loved this activity and remarked on the softness of the feathers—hence Julianne's reference to their 'smooth and soft' feel.)

The Duck

The duck is a lovely bird. Its feet are like flippers.
Its feet help it to swim.
It lives on an island. I like ducks.

RAYMOND, 7

Lyre Bird

Lyre Bird,
lyre bird,
your feathers are beautiful.
You can copy any sound you hear.

KIM, 7

TERM 3: ROCK POOLS AND THE SEASHORE

This museum lecture, the final one for the year, was intensely interesting and instructive. We had taken the whole Infant school for an excursion to Balmoral Beach a few weeks before and children were full of factual information about sea creatures.

In the lecture hall a live sea-horse bobbed about in a glass tank and fascinated all of us. His amazing life history was traced for us and specimens of minute baby sea-horses were shown. Excellent slides highlighted the feeding habits of many other sea creatures. This completed our own study as we were unable to observe this phenomenon at low tide.

The proximity of the mulberry periwinkle to the colony of large barnacles posed a problem which was solved by Timothy, who deduced that the periwinkle must feed upon the tough-looking barnacles. He was right but no one guessed the marvellous detail of the shell-softening acid secreted by the periwinkle.

The limpet was discussed and compared with the land-snail. Is the limpet cemented on to the rock like the barnacle? How does he cling on? Why does he need to cling to the rock? These and many other questions were raised, and nothing was treated superficially. Gradually a definite pattern, extremely fine in detail, was revealed for each little creature.

Children's writing on this occasion was the outcome of their day tour to Balmoral Beach, their study of sea creatures in school, and finally their visit to our Treasure House of Knowledge, to complement, confirm and extend what we had already learnt on this topic.

Notice that our sense games have been effective in making children more aware of their surroundings. For this reason there is delightful sensitivity in this free creative writing.

Balmoral

When I went to Balmoral Beach I felt the wind touching me. The sea smelt salty. I saw an octopus and I knelt to see what was in a rock pool. I heard the waves crashing on the rocks, too.

MICHAEL LO., 7

At the Beach

Listen, I hear a noise from the sea. I hear the crashing of the waves. Look! here are some sea creatures behind a beautiful rock. See the feathery hand stretching out for food. The sea anemone is hungry.

THERESE, 7

The Sea Anemone

Let us go to the rock pool and see the exciting things. Look, I can see a feathery foot moving. I know he is very hungry. I shall feed him. I will give him some shells. He grabs them and closes up to enjoy them.

MARY, 8

38

Balmoral

At Balmoral, Sister fed a sea-flower. His hand came out for the shell. Sister dropped a shell creature in. He caught it and closed his arms around it, and ate it up.

MARK A., 8

The Sponge

We found a sponge. It was like cotton honey-comb. Its colours were orange and yellow. Large sponges that are found in deep seas are used for bath sponges.

KIM, 7

Underwater

There are starfish under the water and many other things, like crabs. We can swim under the sea but we must hold our breath.

GLEN, 7

Sea Creatures

We went to a rock pool and we saw a sea anemone and we fed him. We saw how he shuts his mouth when he eats. When he finishes he opens his mouth for some more.

JULIANNE, 7

The Sea

In the sea the waves go swiftly and roar. When we smell the breeze of the wind it's salty. We notice the flying birds that pass. The sea anemone eats baby shells, and the sun shines above us.

MICHAEL LE., 7

Beach

One day we went to Balmoral Beach. The waves were tumbling on the sand. In some of the rock pools it was calm. The seagulls were flying by. They were flying to the water to get some fish. They were making funny noises.

WADE, 7

The Sea

The sea is sometimes rough and sometimes not. When the sun comes out the sea is sparkling and all sea things are shining brightly.

MARY, 8

The Jellyfish

Jellyfish, Jellyfish you sting everyone. Unlike most fish you have no backbone and cannot be eaten.

KIM, 7

The Waves

Big waves, little waves on the shore, with a crash and boom you pull me down while you pass.

KIM, 7

39

The Sea-Horse

In the museum they have different animals. The sea-horse has a tail curly at the end. It wriggles all the time. The father has a pouch like the kangaroo and he looks after the eggs.

MICHAEL LE., 7

The Sea-Horse

Sea-horse, grey or black,
all day swim along and play.
You are free all day,
so play in May.
Catch your food in May.
On a little weed,
hold on tight in May.
Sea-horse, play all day.

RAYMOND, 7

(The following poem mirrors perfectly the antics of the little sea-horse during our lecture. He bobbed up and down as if for our entertainment. As a contrast to Raymond's carefree abandonment, Patricia's sea-horse is working restlessly and anxiously.)

Sea-Horse

'Sea-horse, sea-horse,
bobbing up and down
maybe you want to have some food today?
Sea-horse, sea-horse
Have you any work?'
'Yes', said the sea-horse,
'I haven't time to play.'
Sea-horse, sea-horse,
bobbing up and down.

PATRICIA, 7

Sea-Horse

The sea-horse floats in the water up and down he goes. He is not very big and he doesn't really look like a horse at all.

MICHAEL L., 7

The Sea-Horse

Twisting and twirling
twisting and twirling,
the sea-horse is moving today.
Twisting and twirling,
twisting and twirling,
all through the day.

CATHERINE, 7

The Sea-Horse

Little sea-horse curling your tail, around a piece of seeweed, you eat prawns.

KIM, 7

Museum

When we went to the museum we saw a film. We saw sea creatures too. There were octopuses, crabs, starfish, sea-horses, and brittle stars too.

MICHAEL LO., 7

Sea-Horse

I saw a sea-horse in a tank. He was swimming around on his tail. He was the father and he has a pouch for the eggs. The teacher feeds him every day.

MICHAEL LO., 7

The Fish

Fish, darting fish, splashing in the sea, they do not die because they have their gills to breathe through.

MICHAEL LO., 7

The Sea

Look, look, look,
at the fish
darting—
in the water
and out of it.

GLEN, 7

The Sea-Horse

A father sea-horse has a pouch. It has baby sea-horses like hairs. The fully grown sea-horses are only about six inches long.

LESLIE, 7

5

With a swing and a ring

'Can you swing me
high in the sky?'
MARK R., 7

AS EARLY AS MARCH this year, I found that children
were writing in rhythmic form with a most poetic style. This usually
happened after a moving personal experience. For example, when a
violent thunderstorm, replete with rocking thunder and electric
lightning-flashes, had shaken Sydney one Saturday evening, children
released their thoughts in creative writing:

> *Stormy Night*
> Stormy night, what do you do?
> I scream with lightning and thunder
> and clear rain too.
> MICHAEL L., 6

(I thought Michael might have meant *clean* in the last line, so I
asked him to explain the word to me. He answered readily, 'Oh, it's
clear, like my glasses.')

> *Storm*
> Did you hear the storm on Saturday night?
> 'Boom!' goes the thunder.
> 'Flash!' goes the lightning.
> 'Crash!' the wind sends a tree over.
> And then what happened?
> What do you think?
> Down came the rain.
> MARK R., 7

At this stage I decided to experiment with the introduction of a
measured rhythm to give all children in the class the *feel* of poetry

and an ability to use it when strong emotion demanded singing words or more moving cadences than prose could provide. As a useful example of concise and disciplined style, I chose the Japanese *haiku* form, some excellent examples of which are to be found in May Hill Arbuthnot's *Time for Poetry*. The *haiku* is a short poem of seventeen syllables set out in three lines. The first line has five syllables, the second seven and the last five. I calculated that the brevity of this form would serve to curtail children's verbosity and make them more conscious of word values and of polished style. No mention was made of rhyme because I wanted the children to avoid sacrificing ideas to weak and often forced rhyme schemes. I read some beautiful examples of *haiku* poems and then children clapped the metre softly. We 'voiced' the rhythm a few times to *la* and studied our examples again. Then children began writing—somewhat timorously at first, but gradually gaining courage and with it insight into word-management. The results were rewarding:

Rainbow

See the rainbow, Tom,
It is red and white and green,
it will go away.

GRANT, 7

Wool

I like sheep's wool Dad,
Sheep's wool makes warm winter coats.
I might buy a coat.

RAYMOND, 7

Soft Wool

The sheep are very soft.
The wool on them is very soft.
I play games with them.

SHARON, 6

Rain

I walk in the rain,
on a winter day with Mum.
The rain goes pit-a-pat.

THERESE, 6

Stars

Can you see the stars,
above me high in the sky?
Softly do they shine.

MARIANNE, 7

43

Trees

I can see the trees
that stretch their branches high above,
and I am down below.

MARIANNE, 7

Hailstorm

There was a lovely moon
and now a hailstorm, do not fear,
for God is in His heaven.

GLEN, 7

My Cat

My cat purrs near me,
He has milk at home with me
when I have my tea.

MICHAEL L., 6

Rain

Softly falls the rain.
It goes pit-pat all day long.
It sounds like a song.

PATRICIA, 7

Rain

I am in the rain.
Softly do I hop in it,
and I like the rain.

PATRICIA, 7

A Bird

Fly, fly, in the sky,
softly I fly in the sky,
and God is high above.

JULIANNE, 6

All children wrote two or three verses in this form. This was enough. There was no need to insist on a rigid metre once the use of rhythmic words was established. Children began quite naturally to suit the form of their work to the subject on which they were writing.

Our first experiment in free verse-making was carried out towards the end of March. It was on the much loved subject of *swinging*. A smooth rhythmic flow befitting the swinging motion characterised all the children's work this day. None of them chose the *haiku* form because it did not suit the action of the swing. I thought that Wade's verse was the most exceptional because his swing mounts so high and then dies down to a veritable standstill:

44

Dying Swing

Swing high into the sky.
Swing swing into the sky,
over the houses high.
Swing high, swing low.
Swing low, low, low
into the grass,
down, down, down into the grass.

WADE, 7

Swing

"Swing, swing
where can you go?'
'High, high,
into the sky and away,
into the sky so high."
'Can you swing me into the sky?"

MARK R., 6

Swinging

'Swing high
up to the sky . . .'
said I.
'I will go swinging
up, up, up . . .'
said I.

MARY, 7

Swing

Swing, swing,
over all things,
like a bird
high up
by the house and trees.

THERESE, 6

Thenceforth topics for verse-making were free. Children were also permitted to use either verse or prose for their diary-writing, and, if appropriate, for their record of lessons. What follows amounts to a small anthology—yet it is only a sample of the prolific writing that poured from the minds and hearts of these Second Grade children.

Bird

Look, look, look,
up in the sky.
A bird is flying
in the sky very high.
The cat will catch it
by the leg,
but the bird will give
the cat a peck.
MICHAEL L., 7

Night

Sleep, sleep, I will go to sleep.
The moon is shining out.
I will have to go to sleep.
Stars are shining out.
CARMEN, 7

Happy Kookaburras

We saw some kookaburras
sitting in a tree
laughing and flying
and singing as loud as could be.
They were dancing and bouncing
all over the tree.
MICHAEL LE., 7

(The word picture of kookaburras 'bouncing' is most apt. This is where children are so delightfully fresh in their approach. I would never have thought of using the word myself.)

By Myself

As I walked by myself
and I talked by myself
I thought about everything
there could be.
Patricia, 7

About this time, summer began to give way to mild autumn days. This was the sunset of the year, the colourful season heralded by so many of the children's poems. Poems there were in abundance, and lilting songs of the wind and the leaves, to keep us in tune with the season. We had also to get out and about to see for ourselves what was happening. Our five Infant classes went together to the Botanical Gardens for a memorable autumn excursion. This was a day filled with important lessons in learning, looking, and listening, but most of all in *belonging* to so beautiful a world.

I know of no place so delightfully situated as our Botanical Gardens, with outlook on the Sydney harbour, with a wide expanse of lawns set with a variety of trees and flowers, with ponds and running water alive with ducks and their young. For many years now, the curator of the Gardens had provided a gardener to explain the wonders of nature to the Grade 2 children. He always gathered some specimens of berries, leaves, or seeds for us to examine closely. This year I asked, in addition, for a rose. Imagine my surprise and the children's joy when, at the end of the day, the gardener gave us not one rose but *one each*. These little city children squealed with delight, 'ooh-hed' and 'ah-ed' buried their faces in the perfumed softness and stroked the velvet petals. It is no wonder then that poetic thought resulted, thoughts indicative of these children's sensitivity to the beauties of nature.

The Rose

Rose, rose,
why do you hurt me with your thorns?
You are red and small.
You are not like a tree,
and you are not a tree.

MICHAEL L., 6

Rose

I am a little rose.
Did you know that I had
a little perfume?

THERESE, 6

Roses

Sometimes a rose is white or red.
The petals are velvety.
They can grow in gardens,
old pots,
or old tins.
I wish I had a rose,
that was a very lovely red.

CATHERINE, 7

The Rose

So lovely is the rose
that has red and golden petals.
It grows with thorns,
even baby roses have thorns.

MARK R., 6

47

A Rose

Softly falls the petal
of a rose,
softly, softly,
falling down,
falling down, down, on the ground.

RAYMOND, 7

Roses

There are roses in my garden,
I have a dog
that likes to tear roses apart,
but I will not let him get them.
I will lock him up in his house,
and the roses will be fresh.

MARIANNE, 7

About Autumn

Autumn leaves come falling down.
They are all brown.
Some get burnt and some don't,
and they fall down one at a time.

MICHAEL LE., 7

Leaves

'Leaves, do you fly all day?'
'Yes we do,
we fly in the sky
and in the street.
We fly all over the town.'

ANTHONY, 7

Leaves

The autumn leaves
are falling down,
falling down so lightly
because they are so soft.

TIMOTHY, 6

Leaves

See the leaves
Yellow and brown,
See them trampled all over the town.
They look like smoke
when they touch the ground.
But mostly they twist
all around.

MARIANNE, 7

Autumn Season

Autumn is here
and the leaves are dancing
all over the street.
Some are twisting and twirling
above me.

KIM, 7

Autumn

Wind makes the leaves blow everywhere,
along the roads and streets.
They are red, yellow, orange and gold.
They make a carpet along the streets.

MARY, 7

Leaves

Leaves, leaves, what do you do?
I flutter and dance all day.
I flutter all over the town.
The day is cold and I fall.

ANTHONY, 7

Autumn

I sit down by the tree
and see the leaves
dropping down
off the tree
and they dance
around my feet.

SILVANA, 7

Wind

I saw the wind
go out one day.
It moves away fast.
It makes a lot of noise,
when it glides and flutters.

THERESE, 6

Wind

'Wind, wind, what do you do?'
'I blow your hats and trees too.
I rattle your windows and doors too.'

ANTHONY, 7

Wind

I went to school on a windy day.
The wind was whistling and twirling.
Then, what do you think?
What happened?
My hat went tearing down the street.

GLEN, 7

Wind

Wind, wind
push the air into the sky.
Into the parachute
the air will go,
over the sky
and into the sails.

CLAUDIO, 7

The Leaves

Yellow and brown,
leaves fall
all over the town.
Every day
I see them fall,
and when the man comes,
he will burn them up,
and I will see the blue smoke
twirl round and round.

JULIANNE, 6

(This is a beautiful verse for so young a child. Though the opening lines vaguely suggest a known poem, still they are presented in a new form with a quiet thought-pattern sustained throughout. The measured rhythm, the directness, sincerity, and utter simplicity are most commendable.)

Towards the end of Term I we took children to see the film *Mary Poppins*. They delighted in the fantastic beauty, the catchy songs, and the refreshing story. How much they enjoyed this outing is reflected in their writing which, again, is poetic:

Mary Poppins

Over the roof
it is dark and black.
I wish we could go on a roof-top
to see the lovely moon,
and the lovely sunset
all blue and yellow and green.

MICHAEL L., 6

50

Merry-go-round

Up and down goes the merry-go-round.
Off come the horses
to ride on the ground.

MARK R., 6

Carpet-bag

I wish I had a carpet-bag,
a little magic one.
I could pick out anything.
I wish I could play with it
or get out of it a plane,
a mirror,
or a dress.

CHRISTINA, 7

My Wish

I wish I had a carpet bag,
as big as big can be,
like Mary Poppins' bag
but not so heavy, see,
but for me,
for me.

CARMEN, 7

Night

Night has come
and the park
is full of shadows
and it's very scarey.

KIM, 7

Kite

'Kite, kite, where can you go?'
'If you like,
I can go over the wires
and high, high up to the sky.'

GLEN, 7

Roof-tops

See the roof-tops high.
Gold shines on them in the night.
They are in the sky.

MARK R., 6

(Here Mark reverts to the *haiku* form for a special purpose. This is the first time it has been used by a child since we introduced it in March.)

The Pillow

Every night
I go to sleep.
My pillow is soft
and deep.
My pillow is white
like a shining light.
        MICHAEL L., 6

Wishes

Wishes, wishes,
all day long,
I wish for a song, you see.
I wish all day.
            CARMEN, 7

Fun

In every job that must be done,
You can have lots and lots of fun,
if you only play the game with me,
and then your work will soon be done,
and you can have a lot more fun.
            MARIANNE, 7

(Marianne's own version of this song reveals easy management of words.)

The Chimney

Down dark and black
is a chimney.
Smoke shall come out of it
in the night time.
        MICHAEL L., 6

Before the term finished Michael L. composed two works of quality:

When I go to Sleep

When I go to sleep
I can think of lovely things.
Yes, I can think of anything.
I can think of the world so lovely,
I can think of the moon above me,
I can think of the little stars above too,
Yes, and I can think of you.

Faster than Me

Faster than a car,
faster than a train,
faster than a bomb,
not a car,
not a train,
not a bomb,
but a big, big long ambulance,
rushing and rushing down the street,
rushing and rushing
faster than my little feet.
Yes, faster than my little feet.
MICHAEL L., 6

(It is evident that Michael had absorbed some of the rhythm of R. L. Stevenson's *From a Railway Carriage* which we had studied recently. Yet the little boy has conveyed an original thought and a feeling that is personal.)

TERM 2

This is the winter term with days of frost, of driving rain and cutting winds, yet also days of mellow sun and gentle breezes. Snow does not fall in our city streets. Even in Hobart, Tasmania, much further south, I saw this happen only once in years; but it can be seen and enjoyed in many of our distant hills and mountains. Children continue to respond to language lessons by writing 'with a swing and a ring'.

Winter

Winter is coming.
Winter is cold.
Winter is coming
and winter will go.
CARMELLA, 8

(Carmella is a youthful philosopher who realises how truly 'all things are passing'.)

Leaves in Winter

'Leaves, leaves, what do you do?'
'I flutter and dance all day
I flutter all over the town.
The day is cold and I fall.'
ANTHONY, 7

53

Trees

In the holidays
I saw lovely trees.
They were branching everywhere.
The leaves were gold and brown.

LESLIE, 7

Winter Fire

Can you see the fire?
Red and yellow
Like some wire.
I like red and yellow fire.

MICHAEL L., 7

The Robin

Robin, you fly to the tree
for berries,
you fight for the berries
all the day.
You look as if you were fighting
for a toy horse.
You are red and white and brown,
and you have a tail
like a paint brush.

CLAUDIO, 7

Winter

When I go up into the snow
I wear my waterproof boots,
When I run and jump
my boots go down into the snow.
In the snow
I pick berries.
I see two birds fighting
over one little berry.

MARK A., 7

Berries

See the birds come down,
snatching berries on the ground.
They float down softly
to the ground.

MICHAEL L., 7

Birds

The birds glide from the tree
to pick at the berries
and they snatch
and chirp at them too.

PATRICIA, 7

54

Birds

What's that noise?
That's the noise of the birds
cheeping,
pecking,
snatching, for berries.

MARK R., 7

Berries

Birds, you fight for berries
when it's tea time.
When I see birds
fighting for berries
I can hear them
make a lot of noise.
They pick the berries
from the plants.
Berries are their best fruit.
The berries are as red as red can be.

ANTHONY, 7

Berries

Listen to that sound.
It's the blackbird's sound.
Do you hear them
fighting and quarrelling
about the red-ripe berries?
I am sure they will soon be
good friends again.

MARIANNE, 7

Berries

It is winter.
Nearly all the leaves
are off the trees.
What do I hear?
Birds are fighting
about the berries.
They quarrel and chirp
and it is as noisy
as noisy can be.

CATHERINE, 7

Winter

When I went to the park
one winter's day
I shivered
all the way.
When I got to the park
there was the frost,
I saw it fall
from the trees.
Across the park I go
as the wind will blow.

CHRISTINA, 7

Winter

Winter brings frost
and winter brings snow
and everything is frozen
except me.

KIM, 7

Cold

Cold is the winter.
Frozen is the river
where we walk now.
All the birds
are hurrying
for berries
for their little ones.

THERESE, 7

Winter

It is freezing on the ice
and misty in the night.
I will skate
on the ice so clear.

PATRICIA, 7

Footprints

Frost is like snow.
Your foot leaves footprints.
Mr Frost has put frost on the ground.
This morning I could find my footprints
on the ground.

CARMELLA, 7

Skating

I feel cold.
I wish I could have a run on the ice
in my ice-shoes.
When I skate on the ice
it feels slippery and dangerous.
When the sun comes out
the ice will melt
and turn into water.

CARMELLA, 7

Winter Fun

Couldn't we go out
on a wintry day
running and skating
with joy and happiness,
and we would be covered with frost.

MICHAEL LE., 7

Rain

See the rain
coming down
from the sky above,
big drops,
little drops,
dancing on the ground.

KIM, 7

The Rain

The rain lies on the tree
with water dripping soft and deep.
The mist has vanished
and it's time for me to get up.

MICHAEL L., 7

Rain

Pittery-pattery
goes the rain
as it scatters
falling down
to the ground
into puddles
big and round.

MARK R., 7

Rain

'Rain, rain, what do you do?'
'I will tell you what I do.
Pitter-patter all day through.
Is that all I could tell you?'

YOLANDA, 7

Rain

Down, down, what comes down?
I know!
The rain comes down.
Sometimes we cry.
It is the same as when the rain comes down.
The rain comes down out of a cloud.
The cloud is like our eyes.

THERESE, 7

Rain Song

It's raining today. It's raining today.
The clouds are not fading fast away.
It all happened today. It happened today.
The clouds are not fading fast away.

MARIANNE, 7

The Wind

The wind started blowing
on my way to school.
The trees were swaying
from side to side
and all the birds
were hurrying
to find shelter.

KIM, 7

Leaves

I saw them twirling
round and round
and then they twirled
faster and faster.
Soon they stopped
and didn't go any faster.
They were still.
They were floppy.
They didn't move
because the wind had gone away.

MARY, 7

One wet morning in the middle of June I took a large tuft of
English-grass to school. It was a brilliant green, soft and springy,

showing matted hairs of roots gripping the soil and silvery heads of seed lifting between the blades.

What would children make of this new challenge? For, though we talked about grass, felt it and even smelt it, I gave no related songs, poems or stories. Instead, children were thrown on their own resources to write meaningfully.

Grass

'Grass, grass, what do you do
standing in the sun?'
'I look to the sky all the time.
I look to the side when the winds blow.
I can grow high if the man will not cut me.'
'Grass, you are soft and very green,
you are very green.'

ANTHONY, 7

Grass

Grass, grass,
as we pass
we see you growing
very slowly.
When you get bigger
I will mow you down.
But you will still grow
slower and slower.

(Michael has made good use of a quiet rhythm for these reflective lines, revealing his awareness of nature.)

Grass

Grass, grass, you are so soft.
Grass,
the cows eat you.
Men cut you
and you grow back up.
Grass, you are so green.

MARY, 7

Grass Carpet

Grass you are so soft to sit on.
We can have picnics on you,
can't you see?
You are so smooth.

CARMEN, 7

59

Grass

Some grass is long.
When you sit on it,
it will bend,
but it will not break.
If you pull it all out
then it will break.

GRANT, 7

Grass

I like the grass.
It is so soft.
I can sleep on it
and I can hide
in the tall grass.

HELLIO, 7

Grass

Grass, grass, you are so soft.
You grow so slowly in the park.
Grass, I know that you are soft
even before I sit on you.
In the city
there's lots of grass.

ANTHONY, 7

TERM 3

The third term comes in with the spring. This is the awakening of the year when 'all things shall be new'. Once more a rich treasure of literature and songs is at hand for our plundering. I love the enthusiastic way seven-year-olds respond to Eleanor Farjeon's delightful spring lyrics, to Christina Rossetti's quietly beautiful lines or to the discussion of an interesting spring picture. This is the time for another excursion to see the changing world. Mere words cannot describe the luminous quality of the oak tree's vibrant green, or the delicate drifting of blossom petals on to the grass. But once children are aware of what the world holds for them, then they, in very truth, inherit their land.

Spring

Don't you see the leaves are out
ready to begin a new life,
ready to look beautiful again?
Every springtime it will begin.
It's new life.

THERESE, 7

Little Flower

Little flower, little flower,
sleeping in the darkness,
When the sun comes
you will rise
to make the day lovely.

CATHERINE, 7

Spring

Spring, spring,
coming in early morning.
The stars are gone.
The birds are singing
to you and to me they sing.

CARMELLA, 7

Trees in Spring

The trees above are so bare
all winter through
but in spring
many green buds appear.

KIM, 7

Spring

In spring
lots of flowers grow,
some white, some pink.
I pick them
when they're fully grown.
They've a lovely perfume.

SHARON, 7

Spring

Come out, little birds
Spring is here.
Come out
come out and sing.
Don't you know
spring is here?

PATRICIA, 7

Spring

The little green buds
are peeping out
like a little green sprout.
They will grow
They will grow
a new leaf.
Wouldn't you like to be a bud?
I would.

MICHAEL L., 7

61

Spring

When it is spring
I sing in the sun,
I sing in my home.
I sing in the rain
with my rain coat
and my rain hat on,
and I sing in the wind.
CLAUDIO, 7

Birds in Spring

They glide and flutter
round the place.
I peep from behind the curtain
and watch them.
But if they see me
they will be shy
and fly away.
MARY, 7

Signs of Spring

I've seen signs of spring.
I've seen blossoms out.
I've seen green buds on trees,
and at school,
I've seen our plant
with a new spring-green leaf.
RAYMOND, 7

Spring

Spring!
You sun the trees
and sap the leaves.
It's time to splash and play.
Though that you are very cool,
I like you every day.
MATTHEW, 7

Walking

Under the trees we walk
with stones beneath our feet.
The sun shines through the trees,
little round circles shaking,
because the wind is blowing.
MARY, 7

Country Lane

A walk in a country lane,
the fragrance of the flowers
flying in the wind.
The shade of trees
cooling me.
The insects flying above my head.
Then ants marching across my toes
while I am sitting under the tree.

MICHAEL L., 7

Country Lane

The wind is blowing.
The flowers are growing.
Is is fresh today.
The poppies are coming out.
The perfume of the wild rose is in the air.
It's peaceful and quiet.
The bird is flying near the corners,
having a look for cobwebs for its nest.

BRETT, 7

The Country Lane

How nice to be there!
You will walk so smoothly and gently.
You will see a feathered bird gliding through,
and you see him going to his nest.
You see poppies and insects all about you.
Then under a shady tree you sit,
seeing all the little things everywhere.

JOSEPHINE, 6

Country Lane

I skip,
I run,
and I see pretty flowers.
The sun
is shining so beautifully
and the sky is going round.
and round,
and round.
I love the flowers
and the sun
and the sky too.
Everything is beautiful
in the country lane.

STEPHEN, 7

63

Country Lane

Rose, let me smell your perfume.
Let me feel your pink petals.
And when the wind will come,
you will dance and dance
under the moon.

VIVIANNA, 7

Country Lane

There are roses in the country lane.
There are shaggy trees with green leaves on them.
I wish I lived in the country lane.
There would be no traffic
and you could go for walks there.

FRANKA, 7

The Willow Tree

I am a sad little willow tree.
My leaves droop down into the water,
but other trees have their leaves up
and they are as stiff as a pin.

CHERYL, 7

Daffodil

Little daffodil,
you are opening, opening,
and now you are free.
Before you were closed, closed,
oh so tight.
You are coloured with yellow, yellow,
oh so beautifully coloured with yellow.

ANNE, 7

Leaf

If I were a leaf
I would drift down so slowly to the ground,
you would think I was a parachute
or a fairy.

STEPHEN, 7

As a contrast to the description in Chapter Three of the butterfly that emerged from the pupa case one April, the one described here was long awaited and did not emerge until August.

The Butterfly

For now we have waited all winter long for this little old butterfly to come out of his pupa-case, and fly around for us.

KAREN, 6

64

▶'. . . it's beautiful!' Glen examines
our newly-emerged Blue Fanny Butterfly.

▼Children study sea-creatures in school.
Julianne examines the egg of a Botany
Bay shark which we found on Balmoral
Beach.

▼We had to get out and about to see for ourselves what was happening. A group of children sketching the ducks in the Gardens.

▲Spring is the time for another excursion to see the changing world, Catherine peeps into the nest of a Silver-eye in Centennial Park.

The Pupa-Case

Open, open, pupa-case!
If you will open,
you will have coloured wings
and you will stretch and stretch
and come out of your little house.

PHILOMENA, 7

The Pupa-Case

Look at me! Look at me!
I am like poppies coming out from their barley bed.
I split open the chrysalis, and I come out
like a fairy in the moonlight.

CHERYL, 7

Butterfly

When we said to the butterfly,
'Come out!'
It would not come out.
Only when it is God's time
it will come out with its coloured wings.

CHARLES, 8

Little Butterfly

'Little butterfly, little butterfly,
all crumpled up.
You have been asleep
all winter long.
Will you soon awaken?'
'Yes, I might awaken now.'
Wait! Listen!
'Crack, crack!'
goes the chrysalis.
Then, a little yawn:
'Ah! Ah!'
Now he is out.
Oh isn't that nice!
Now he is stretching his wings,
and another little yawn:
'Ah!' ...
Then he said,
'At last I am awake,
and look at my colourful wings.
Now I will suck up some nectar.'

PETA, 7

Butterfly

Come out! Come out,
sweet butterfly!
You come out with your crumpled wings.
Then you swift out and fly.
Soon you will stretch your gleaming tongue
and look for nectar.

MATTHEW, 7

Buds

Some buds are sticky
some are not.
They open so slowly
and they grow so slowly.
When some of them open
they will be flowers.
I will pick them for my Mother.

CLAUDIO, 7

Bees

See the bees come hurrying by
using their sucking tubes
to get nectar.
'Buzz! buzz!'
That's all we hear.
Buzz buzz little bees.

GLEN, 8

Marianne has a real gift for rhythmic words. Her handwriting is
scrawly because her ideas come faster than she can set them down;
and she is always writing, as if her thoughts are demanding an
outlet. Of all the children she is the most consistent and prolific
writer:

Bees

Bees, bees,
buzzing in and out
through the flowers and all about.
come, come,
come and see
come and see my cherry tree.

Plants

Plants, plants,
shining in the night
and shining in the morning
and shining in the light.
I love you little plants,
shining in the morning,
and shining in the night.

66

Blossoms

Pretty blossoms
come out today.
Come out! Come out!
come out if you may.
Pretty blossoms
come out today.

Spring

Birds, come out
Spring is here.
Come out and sing
do not fear.
Come out and be happy.
Don't you know
that Spring is here?

Trees

Isn't it fun to look at a tree.
Can't you see? Can't you see?
Wouldn't you want to climb a tree.
It would be fun.
Can't you see?

MARIANNE, 7

I have already described in Chapter Two (*Natural Science*) how vocabulary was built up for creative writing on the topic of the *Snail*. Most children freely responded to this subject in verse rather than prose.

A Snail

Slowly, slowly, down the path
goes a slippery slimer,
leaving a silver trail.
Very, very slowly down the path
goes a slippery snail.

RAYMOND, 7

The Snail

Snail you walked on the footpath.
You left a silver trail.
I follow your trail of silver
Sometimes I find you.

HELLIO, 7

(This is a wonderful effort for a Spanish boy with little command of English.)

The Snail

I see some silvery stuff.
What can it be?
It shines like gold.
Oh what can it be?
It's going to my steps.
It is a snail.
                    JULIANNE, 7

Snail

Who left that silver trail?
Who left that silver trail?
Who left that silver trail?
It must have been a snail.
                    CATHERINE, 7

Snails

Snails have shells
and they can go
inside and go out.
They're crawling slowly
stretching out,
crawling slowly
stretching out.
I like snails
moving slowly
and stretching out.
                    MARIANNE, 7

Snail

Snail! Snail!
Leaving a silver track,
never mind how slow you seem.
You and I are friends, you see.
                    MARK R., 7

Snail

Wouldn't you like to be a snail,
and make a golden track?
Wouldn't you like to have a home up
upon your back?
Wouldn't you like to have antennas
with a tiny shiny eye?
                    TIMOTHY, 6

(This echoes the beginning of G. Dearmer's poem *Whale* which
Timothy always liked. He has made use of the same metre and
opening phrase but the ideas are all his own.)

The Snail

The snail goes slowly
down the path,
leaving a silver trail.
When danger is near
he pops into his shell
and doesn't come out
until it is clear.

KIM, 8

The Snail

When I went out
I saw a horn-nosed monster.
Away he went
leaving a silver trail.
'Oh you silly thing'
said I,
'it is a snail.'

RAYMOND, 7

In October the children enjoyed a new language activity: painting pen portraits of people familiar to them. Most of these were written in rhythmic form:

My Father

My father is like a pine.
He is so tall and friendly.
He calls me and hugs me and says
'You are mine.'

MARIANNE, 7

My Friend

My friend is tall
and always bossy.
When she is angry
she yells out with a roar.
She oftens tells me
to go to bed
when it's only six-o-clock.

KIM, 7

Guess Who?

She said, 'Get up, let's play!
We'll play the trumpet.
We'll play the drum.
We'll play as loud as we can.'
That's my sister.

CATHERINE, 7

69

My Father

My father is strong, happy and thoughtful.
He works fast and swiftly, and he obeys.
My father loves me, talks to me and works every day

MICHAEL LE., 7

My Brother

My brother is always running round.
You think he's never sitting down.
Any time you want to watch TV,
he's up and down, you see.

THERESE, 7

My Mother

My mother is always crying
because I get sick.
I wake in the night
with a terrible fright
and I start crying too.
Then I become scared
and run to my Mother's bed
and tell her what happened
in my dream.

CARMEN, 7

My Mother

She's always in a hurry,
goes shopping
comes back and cooks.
When I need her
she always is ready for me.
When we go to a party
she's always ready before me.

MARY, 8

Friends

If I go anywhere
my friend will go with me.
We stay together
and play together.

WADE, 7

My Mum

My mum goes to work.
She bakes cakes,
then she comes home and does more work.
She helps me with my homework,
and then goes to work again.

MARK A., 7

70

My Father

My father is a cheerful fellow.
He is as big as a pine.
He always tries to be on time.
He's a fine man.

MARK R., 7

My Father

My father is big.
He smokes a pipe,
and sometimes
he grows bigger and bigger

ROBERT, 8

Early in November I told children an aboriginal folk tale about
two lizards called Wo-wo-loo and Walla-wid-bit. Each of them
could do a fascinating dance. The aborigines asked the lizards to
teach them and they complied, and when the two dances were
woven together, a new dance was made which they called *Mundi-wah*.
Some delightfully rhythmic songs emanated from this story.

Aborigines

Mu, mu, mundi-wah
ha, ha mundi-wah
mundi-, mundi-wah
as we dance around the fire
we dance our own corroboree.
Walla-wid-bit and Wo-wo-loo
taught us. Won't you join in too?
Ha, ha, mundi-wah.

MARIANNE, 7

The Lizards

Wo-wo-loo was a frilled lizard
Walla-wid-bit was a blue-tongue.
They each had a dance,
Ha, ha, clap, clap, clap,
ha, ha, turn around click.
Ha, Ha, mundi-wah!

GRANT, 7

The Corroboree

'Aborigines, look, look, look!
Two lizards do fine steps.'
'Do teach us.'
Wo-wo-loo said 'Yes'.

71

'Now, now, now,
we do corroboree.
Paint ourselves white.
Wo-wo-loo,
Walla-wid-bit,
join us for Mundi-wah'
                              RAYMOND, 7

                              Corroboree

Woo-wah
woo-wah!
Wo-wo-loo and Walla-wid-bit
are two different lizards.
Two aborigines are watching
and they say
'Could you teach us
that corroboree?'
So they named it the Mundi-wah,
and the tribe is doing it now.
                              MICHAEL LO., 7

                              Aborigines

Aborigines saw Wo-wo-loo
and Walla-wid-bit
dancing together.
'Wo-wo-loo will you teach us that dance?
It will do for our corroboree.
We will call it Mundi-wah.'

                    A Song for a Corroboree

Ai, ar, you, lar, wa!
We are having a corroboree.
Two lizards are joining in.
One's name is Wo-wo-loo.
He's very clever indeed.
The other is Walla-wid-bit.
They could do very fine steps,
twisting and twirling,
jumping and hopping.
When they had finished
the aborogines said
'Do teach us!'
They said 'Yes'.
'Ai, ar, you, lar, wa!
We will call it Mundi-wah.'
                              KIM, 7

72

Aborigines' Song

'Waa, yaa, yaa, yaa!'
I see two lizards dancing there.
One named Wo-wo-loo
and one Walla-wid-bit.
The aborigines said,
'Will you teach us that dance?'
They answered 'Yes', and they did.
They called it 'Mundi-wah'
'Waa, yaa, yaa, yaa!'

SHARON, 7

Corroboree

They dance their own corroboree
'Oo, soo, hoo, hoo.'
Walla-wid-bit taught them,
So did Wo-wo-loo.
They clash their sticks
'Oo, soo, hoo, hoo!
You can do it too.

MARIANNE, 7

Wo-wo-loo

'Wo-wo-loo, Wo-wo-loo
dance a corroboree
of your own.
Get some friends
Wo-wo-loo,
they can do it with you too.
Wo-wo-loo, Wo-wo-loo.
Walla-wid-bit
Walla-wid-bit
Yah, yah, yah!
Mundi-wah!

MARY, 7

The Lizards

Wo-wo-loo and Walla-wid-bit
each made up a dance.
Stamp, kick and swish your tail.
'Can you teach us?'
'Wia, woo, loo, loo,
Yah, lah, aah',
they sang at their corroboree.
They dance the Mundi-wah.
Frilly lizard Wo-wo-loo
and Bluey-tongue Walla-wid-bit,
know every bit of it.
'Wia woo lo loo
Yah lah aah!'

MARK R., 7

73

Corroboree

'Walla-wid-bit
Jump up high.'
'Ah! ah!
Mundi-wah!'
'Wo-wo-loo
join in too.'
'Ah! ah!
Mundi-wah!'
'Dance, jump, twist around,
jump straight off the ground.'
'Ah! ah!
Mundi-wah!'

PATRICIA, 7

(Of all these exciting aboriginal rhythms we found that Patricia's was most suitable for singing and that its short lines and haunting refrain made it the most effective for a native dance.)

Towards the year's end some delightful sea verses were written, inspired no doubt by our visit to Balmoral Beach and our detailed study of this topic.

Waves

Waves roaring,
waves splashing,
waves eating the rocks,
where deep in a rock pool
A sea-flower is sucking its food.

RAYMOND, 7

Calm

The water is calm today,
the water is calm today.
It feels like a very soft feather.
The water is calm today.

CATHERINE, 7

Waves

The sounds
of the sea
are nice sounds
on the shore.
They wash
the loose shells
off the rocks.
The waves
have lovely sounds.

MICHAEL L., 7

The Sea

Waves go over and over
Splash! Shwish!
go the waves.
But when the waves stop
it is as still as glass.
I look into a rock pool,
deep, deep,
into a rock pool.

PATRICIA, 7

Sea Creatures

Little tiny sea creatures
everywhere you go
I can see you so.
Mother said 'They smell.'
Baby said he likes them.
Father said 'Get them out!'

THERESE, 7

Again it was Marianne who dashed off verses that were full of onomatopoeia, deftly chosen rhythm, and childlike gaiety:

The Sea

'Be a little friendly', said me.
'No, no', said the sea.
'I want to clash my jaws
and break the rock.'
'O won't you be a little friendly?'
'Can't you see?
I have no time to be,
no time to be.'

The Waves

The waves of the sea
will tip-toe away.
Yes, they may,
Yes, they may.
Tip-toe away
tip-toe away.
Or what if you are in the surf?
The waves will rush to you
and come on top of you
Hush, rush,
hush, rush,
hush, rush, they may.

75

Sea Creatures

Creatures, creatures, in the sea
I am here and God made thee.
You may not be His child,
but He is gentle and mild,
gentle and mild,
gentle and mild to you and me.

MARIANNE, 7

Sea

Sea,
you thrash yourself
on hard dry rocks,
and your spray flies high
like a bird in the sky.
You gnash your teeth
with a swishing sound,
and you curl yourself
round . . . round . . . round.

MICHAEL L., 7

The Beach

I felt that the sea was spitting at me,
and I felt so cool
as the sea was pushing itself up to me.

STEPHEN, 7

Sea

When it is raining
the sea is all grey.
It rocks like a rocking chair
all the day.
Rock, rock, sea,
and be very grey.

FRANKA, 7

Sea

Sea,
you make a pool
and you curve the pool so high,
it nearly touches the sky.

BERNICE, 7

Seaweed

Oh Seaweed,
curling and moving around,
you wish you could be free.
You would like
to walk and walk
above the surface of the sea.

ANNE, 7

76

Sea Weed

Weeds dripping,
weeds slipping,
weeds falling,
weeds crawling,
down, down, into the water.
Then they stretch their arms
out, out, into the air.

CHERYL, 7

Seagull

Seagull, seagull,
flying through the air so freshly
and going everywhere you want to go.
I wish I was a seagull
so that I could go everywhere I want to go.

ANTON, 7

Sea Creatures

The periwinkle does not swim, but the octopus does.
The starfish attaches itself to a rock
and remains there until it is ready to eat.

STEPHEN, 7

The Jingle Shell

Jingle shell! Jingle shell!
You glitter so brightly in the sun.
You are orange with shining nacre.
You are cool and so refreshing.

ANNE, 7

Shells

Shells are like people in a slight way.
They get their food from the sea, we sometimes do too.
This is how they get their food:
Their door opens, and the feathery feet spread out
to catch the watery food.
The waves shrivel away,
then the shell waits for another wave.

MICHAEL, 7

The Sea

The sea splashes and clashes
against the rocks.
He chews the rocks
and rolls on the tide,
and when he is finished
he calms down inside.

STEPHEN, 7

All the little shells
marching in a row,
'Sloosh, sloosh, sloosh,'
on their little feet they go.
They come to me and smile at me,
as they walk along.
They always have a smiling face
when they walk along.
'Sloosh, sloosh, sloosh.'

With these verses of the sea I close this discussion of 'words with a ring and a swing', but for the children it is far from closed. The experience has opened wide the avenue of verse-making which these boys and girls will be found using again and again. In writing verse themselves, children have developed an awareness of the possibilities of words to create movement, melody, and atmosphere. They listen to poetry reading more readily, exercising their auditory and visual imagery with keen perceptual awareness while responding to the kinaesthetic element, or the rhythm of the lines. But both the writing of verse and the appreciation of poetry have an even more far-reaching effect on our children. May Hill Arbuthnot deftly explains that poetry carries the child 'from skips and gallops, to the world of dreams and aspirations', She affirms that time spent on poetry is essential and that it 'should be a time to lift your spirits and give them something to grow on'.

6

We look and learn

'I see people
pulling cotton . . .'
CATHERINE, 7

OUR REGULAR school television programme was referred to in Chapter 2 as an effective means of vocabulary enrichment. After each programme, thematic word-lists were compiled in order to establish children's inner criteria and also to give them a useful reference for creative writing. This became, at the end of Stage 3 of Words in Colour, free creative writing because the children were then able to use any sign on the Fidel and to formulate any English word. Given stimulating topics at this stage, the children advanced rapidly in the art of writing, as the following examples show:

TERM 1

Landforms

A hill is like a camel's hump. When I go to school I run to the hill. I walk up the hill slowly at first. Then I run down as fast as can be.

CHRISTINE, 7

About Landforms

The hills are very hard to walk up. The land has a bay and a river. The valley is low and it has a canal.

MICHAEL LE., 7

Milk

Early each morning I go out and get the milk from the cows. I put it outside the door for the milkman to come and take it. It's getting dark now and I shall leave my cows.

MARIANNE, 7

79

Milk

One day at school we saw milk. It was fresh, just from the cows. We even saw little pigs. It was a beautiful sight to see.

THERESE, 6

Dairy Farm

We get milk from the dairy farm. The cows are milked by machine and then the milk is put into buckets and sent out to the factories.

PATRICIA, 7

Dairy Farm

Michael went for a holiday to a dairy farm. The farm was not so big at all. Michael milked the cows. After milking he gave the calves and pigs skim-milk, but he only gave the dog a pat.

CARMEN, 7

The Snail

The snail has no backbone but has a hard shell to keep it from harm.

KIM, 7

Vertebrates

Birds have backbones and people too. They have big bones. Big things have bones. You can walk and jump because you have bones. If you pick an animal up you will feel its bones.

MICHAEL LE., 7

Invertebrates

Invertebrates are animals without backbones. Men have backbones. Some animals have no backbones.

LESLIE, 7

Snails

Snails have no bones. The inside of them is soft. They are invertebrates and they have a hard shell too.

CATHERINE, 6

The Starfish

Starfish, starfish, you are lovely.
When you have a broken leg, you can repair it.

ROBERT, 7

Starfish

'Starfish, starfish,
what do you do
under the water
all day through?'
'I stick to the rocks
as hard as I can
so that no one will hurt me.'

CATHERINE, 6

80

Starfish

I saw a starfish repair its leg. Sometimes people take its leg off to see it being repaired. A starfish takes three days or more to grow a new leg.

CARMELLA, 8

Living Things

Elephants, snakes, fish, ants, and kangaroos are
living things.
Rocks are not living things
You are a living thing.
I am a living thing.
Every man and woman is a living thing.

RAYMOND, 7

TV

We went to TV today and we liked it. It was about living things. A rock is a non living thing. It can't move or grow or eat. A kangaroo is a living thing. It's different from the rock.

MARK R., 6

Plants

Plants make their own food. But how do they get their food? Water, air, and sun make their food. It is a kind of sugar. But it is not the sugar we eat.

CARMEN, 7

TERM 2

Jointed-Legged Animals

A spider is in a group called jointed-legged. There are many more in this group; ants, bees, and butterflies are some of them.

MARK R., 6

About Armour

The armour of the foot can move.
I had armour on one day,
and I walked in it.
I could move my elbow in it too.

MICHAEL LB., 7

A Knight

I wish I was a knight. My suit would be like bones because the chest and arms and feet would move too.

ANTHONY, 7

Sting-ray

Sting-ray, sting-ray
why do you sting the people,
when they go near you?
You are like a jelly-blubber.

CATHERINE, 7

81

Flying Fish

The flying fish has wings so that it can fly. When it lands it splashes in the water. It is a vertebrate with a backbone. It eats different kinds of fish.

MICHAEL LE., 7

Fish

There are many kinds of fish at the bottom of the sea. There are some flying fish. Some are very little and they swim very fast.

MARY, 8

Invertebrates

Invertebrate animals have no bones. Some are dangerous, some aren't. The octopus and the squid haven't bones. They are called invertebrate animals. That means they have no bones. Some animals have bones and they are called vertebrate animals.

MARK R., 6

Microscope

One day I went to the seaside.
I saw many fishes.
You need a microscope to see some of them.
They are very small and interesting.

TIMOTHY, 6

Sea Star

At the beach I saw a sea star. It was shaped like a real star in the sky. Its colour was grey.

SILVANA, 7

Molluscs

On TV we saw invertebrates called molluscs. Some are snails. Snails have different shapes of shells.

MARK A., 8

Molluscs

A snail is in a group called molluscs. Many more are in this group. The octopus is the best thing. They are invertebrates.

MARK R., 6

Molluscs

Some molluscs have a shell and some do not. But people have no shells on their backs. Some animals have a shell. But a tiger or a cat have no shells on their backs.

ANTON, 7

The Snail

Snails have feelers. If you touch them they will go back into their shells, but soon they will come out again.

GRANT, 7

Shells

There are many kinds of shells. Some are at the bottom of the water. Some are stuck on the rocks. Sometimes I try to get shells off the rocks but I cannot because they are stuck on so hard.

MARY, 8

Invertebrates

I have a backbone but a starfish has not. There are many animals that have no backbones. They are called invertebrates.

SHARON, 7

The Baker

Who makes the bread? The Baker. But where does he get the wheat? From the farm of course. It has a big field to plough for the wheat. And now the farmer is ready to get the flour in a big truck and take it to every baker in town.

THERESE, 6

Wild Horse

Wild horse, wild horse,
zooming away,
tell me why you race all the day?
I race and run with my head up high
and my mane is flying in the sky.
I am so wild and rough and free.
This is the life that is meant for me.

PETA, 7

Wild Horse

I am a wild horse.
I thunder along the dusty track.
My tail flashes by. My mane flies.
I stampede across the dewy grass early in the morning.
My tail slaps against the other horses' bodies
and when the sun shines
my yellow skin will gleam like a sparkling river.

MICHAEL L., 7

Horse

The horse goes roaring on the track.
With a great big stamp he flashes through the meadow.
He's bucking as high as the sky.
He's flying through the swifting clouds.
The stallion is his name.
With his great big muscles he thunders through the stampede.

MATTHEW, 7

Horses

We are horses
galloping,
galloping and running,
and running over the hills
and far away.
Our tails go swish!
swash!
in the breeze.

ANNE, 7

Sunraysia

At Sunraysia it is sunny because the sun is up every day. Grapes grow there and fruit grows too. But how do they grow? Well, sun helps and water too. But how do they get their water? Well, I hope it rains on them soon.

CARMEN, 7

Vineyards

Grapes grow in vineyards. Our main vineyards are in South Australia. From the crushed grapes wine is made. We also get sultanas and raisins from grapes.

KIM, 7

Cotton

I see people pulling cotton from the cotton flower. It is fresh and white and very soft.

CATHERINE, 7

Cotton

Cotton grows on a plant. When the pods burst the cotton is ready to be picked. Cotton is made into many types of cloth.

KIM, 7

Plants

I have many plants. Would you like to see them? Here is a fir tree. If snow gets on it, it will soon slip off. I have some ferns too. Here is a fish-bone fern, and here is a corn seed. You can learn a lot about plants from TV.

MARIANNE, 7

Plants

Plants, plants, you are
wide and strong, opening in summer
and closing in winter.

CARMEN, 7

84

Trees

Oh, is the new tree here?
Yes, yes look!
Here it is!
The branches have started to show the leaves.

THERESE, 7

Mosses and Cones

Moss grows in shady places. You will find that moss is slippery. Sometimes you will see moss growing on trees. You will find that seeds fall out of the cones. The red-wood is the biggest tree in the world.

RAYMOND, 7

Spring

Spring is here at last
and all my seeds will grow into flowers.
I will take some to school.

WADE, 7

Cones

In the cone there are seeds. When a seed falls from a tree the roots of the seed will go down to the bottom of the ground. The little tree grows. When the tree is big another cone will grow.

HELLIO, 7

Ferns

There are many kinds of ferns, thin ones, short ones, and long ones. The most famous fern is the fish-bone fern.

KIM, 7

Nut

See a nut grow into a tree.
A nut is a seed.
Then it grows into a tree.

TIMOTHY, 6

The Bush

In the bush you will find many wild flowers. You'll find mosses too. I have two of my friends here, Cathy and Kim. Kim wanted to go on the mosses but she slipped over. Cathy found a lizard. She knows she mustn't touch it.

MARIANNE, 7

(In this space age, it is to be expected that even seven-year-olds will be intensely interested in natural phenomena such as the earth as part of the universe, time, climate and weather. Children's writing reveals their involvement in the pattern of Natural Science.)

The World

In the world around us there are many strange things, and a lot of planets and men go up in space ships to look at the moon.

GLEN, 7

Volcano

The volcano's lava is very hot. If the hot lava touches you, you will be burnt, and the sore will hurt. So don't go near a volcano.

MARY, 8

Lava

Lava is very hot. It can melt rocks. Lava comes from volcanoes. The lava comes out when the volcanoes explode.

CARMELLA, 7

The Volcano

The volcano has hot lava. If hot lava touches you, you will be burnt and it will sting very much. Hot mud is just as bad. It will hurt too. So don't go near hot mud or a volcano.

ANTONY, 7

Planet Venus

The planet Venus is the same size as the moon. Venus and the moon have not very much gravity because they are much smaller than the earth. The moon is only half the size of the earth.

ANTONY, 7

Sun to Moon

'Moon, moon, don't stand in front of me. I am shining to the earth with my light pointing down.' (If the moon stands in front of the sun it is called an eclipse.)

CARMEN, 7

The Volcano

One day I went for a trip, far, far away. I saw a volcano. Some lava came out of it. The lava burnt flowers, trees and everything around.

ROBERT, 7

TERM 3

Time

Have you ever noticed how time flies? It seems as if two weeks is an hour.

MARK R., 7

Day and Night

On the other side of the world it is dark and in Sydney it is daytime. But tonight it will be dark here and on the other side of the world it will be light.

TIMOTHY, 7

The World

The world spins and spins. All places get light and dark in turn. The world spins and spins and spins.

WADE, 7

The World

The world goes round and round. While I'm asleep and while I'm awake the world never stops spinning.

KIM, 7

The Earth

The earth spins round and round the sun. The sun shines down and gives us light. Sometimes the sun rises at 6 o'clock.

ANTONY, 7

The World Around Us

The world around us is a lovely sight. There are mountains, stars, sun and planets. There are clouds, rivers, deserts and the moon.

MICHAEL LO., 6

The World

The world is made for us. On the face of the world is Australia. It is the best place in the world. There are rivers and everything here.

PATRICIA, 7

Sun

The sun does not move. The world moves around the sun. It moves around and around. If one side of the world is facing the sun it is daytime. If the other side of the world is facing the sun it is night-time.

CATHERINE, 7

The Lightning

The lightning is very white. It flashes like a hand on the tree. If it rains you can see the lightning and you can hear the storm. When it stops you can't hear the lightning or the storm any more.

JULIANNE, 6

The Mountains

Mountains so tall and blue
reaching for the sky.
You are so steep,
it will be hard for people to climb you.

KIM, 7

The World

In leap year there are 366 days. In a year there are 365 days. Sometimes the sun sets at 6.25 p.m. The world moves around the sun and it spins around itself all the time.

CATHERINE, 7

87

The Earth

We live on the earth. It is very dark underneath, away from the sun. If you really want to know what the earth is, well, it is soil. If you put a seed in, it will grow in a few days.

JULIANNE, 7

The Moon

When the earth goes around the sun once, it is one year and all the time, the moon goes round the earth. Tonight you cannot see the moon. In a telescope you can see the moon. There will be a full moon on Friday.

RAYMOND, 7

The Weather

The weather can change very quickly. Today it could be hot and tomorrow it could rain. The air all round Sydney is warm, but the air in the Arctic and the Antarctic is cold, because the Arctic is at the top and the Antarctic at the bottom of the world.

ANTONY, 7

Weather

Hurricanes can cause damage to your home. One day it blew a home far far away. A lot of people were killed. A lot more people were sick. The hurricane never came again.

WADE, 7

The Weather

When the wind blows a boat 5 miles an hour, it doesn't go very fast. When it blows 15 miles an hour it goes faster. When it goes 50 miles an hour it goes much faster. When it goes 75 miles an hour it is a hurricane.

JULIANNE, 7

Weather

When the wind goes 75 miles an hour it is a hurricane. At 50 miles an hour it will damage boats. The clouds bring water to the earth.

GLEN, 7

Weather

Weather, weather, when it's cold you blow the trees and strike like lightning. When it's warm you put a glow on the trees. When it's very wintry on the sea you blow the wind at 75 miles an hour and that is called a hurricane. Sometimes, you make me hot and then cold too.

MARY, 7

The Moon

The moon sometimes rises at 6.14 a.m. The earth moves around the sun. Every fourth year is called a leap year.

MARK R., 7

The World

Every morning the sun comes out. In the olden days they thought that the sun turned around the world, but it did not. The world turns around the sun. There is a north pole and south pole too.

RAYMOND, 7

Time

In our country we have a clock to tell the time from. It is summer now. The date is the 19th September. At 9 o'clock it is schooltime. At 11 o'clock it is playtime. We have dinner at half past 12, and we go home at half past 3. We often go to bed at 8 o'clock. Sometimes the moon waxes and at other times it wanes. Every fourth year is a leap year.

KIM, 7

The Calendar

The Calendars have all the months on them. After the moon gets fat it goes skinny again. Monday really means Moonday. Some other months are January and May.

MICHAEL LE., 7

The Earth

The earth is a planet. It spins and moves around the moon. It takes nearly a month for the earth to go around the moon. Men go up in space to learn about the moon. It is wonderful to look at our earth from above.

ANTONY 7

Weather Report

When it is cold you call it min. It is about 40 degrees. When it is hot you call it max. and that is about 60 degrees. There are many kinds of clouds. Rain-clouds are called nimbus-clouds. The white clouds are cumulus and they mean 'no rain' so it will be fine.

SHARON 7

Weather

If the wind is coming from the west, it is called a westerly. If it goes at 75 miles an hour it is called a hurricane. The thermometer tells us the temperature. It may be cold or hot or warm or cool.

RAYMOND, 7

Time and Weather

In South Australia it is very hot at Marble Bar. When winds move they blow westerly, easterly, northerly or southerly. All these clouds have different names, the cumulus, the nimbus and the cirrus. When you want to measure the temperature you need a thermometer.

MICHAEL LE., 7

Weather

Marble Bar is the hottest place in Australia and Mount Kosciusko is the coldest. A slight breeze means a little breeze and a storm cloud is called cumulo-nimbus.

RAYMOND, 7

The Sun

The sun has a very bright shine. You shouldn't look at the sun because it will hurt your eyes. The world moves while the sun shines. If you were in a dark room and had a ball and a torch, you'd be able to put on the torch, and move the ball. It would shine on half the ball at a time, and that is how the sun shines on the earth.

MICHAEL L., 7

River

River falling down the mountainside,
'Swish, splash,
slish, slash,'
running rippling, sliding behind.
You never want to stop, but sometime you will.

MICHAEL L., 7

Boat

Running down
the brown reflected stream
ripples with a shining gleam,
ripples running behind and below
with a little gleaming glow.
The boat is calm.
The stream is quiet.
The martin is gone.
The stars are bright.
The name of the captain is John.

MICHAEL L. 7

The Jenolan Caves

The dripping slipping drops go under and under.
When you go into the Jenolan Caves
you look as tiny as an ant
crawling under a giant pin.
You could sail a plastic boat
under and over
the stalactites and stalagmites
and you might find it
in the sea.

CHERYL, 7

Paper Boats

One, two, three,
little boats
floating down the stream.
One, two, three,
candles all alight.
All in a single line.
All in a single line.

GLEN, 7

90

Letters

Before you post a letter you must put your name, address, street and the State on it. Then put on the stamp and put it in a letterbox. It is taken in a van to the post office sorting room and then off it goes.

RAYMOND, 7

Postman

I am a postman. I get up at 4 o'clock in the morning. I go to the post office to get the letters and I put them into my bag. Then I go and post them. I get out lots of letters. Oh, here is one for Kim.

CATHERINE, 7

Letters

Letters have to go a very long journey. You write a letter. Then you post it and the postman has a clearing. He takes the letters to the big city post office where they are sorted. After that they go to a small office. Then when they have finished everything, the postman delivers the letters.

MICHAEL L., 7

The Postman

The postman goes down the street putting a letter or two in the letter boxes. Our postman's name is Ray. He is very friendly and always says 'Hello'. At Christmas time he is very busy delivering parcels and cards.

KIM, 7

The Policeman

The policeman is a good helper because he gives us directions on the road. He is kind if you are lost and tell him where you live.

PATRICIA, 7

Policeman

When I cross the road I know a policeman will be there. I might be crossing the road and a policeman will be there, there, there, everywhere.

MARY, 8

Our TV lesson on Safety First serves to supplement the regular instructions given each year in our school by trained policewomen. They lecture all classes, implementing safety first techniques and thus helping to prevent accidents. That the teaching has gone home is evident from these extracts from children's writing:

Crossing

When you cross you must not run, and you must push the button if there is one. Be kind and help people across the street as you know hundreds of people are killed. So remember, always help people.

MARIANNE, 7

Safety First

When you cross the road you look to the right, and then you look to the left, and look to the right again, and walk across the road but never run. If you see the light go red and it blinks, you still keep on walking to the other side. When you get off a bus do not ever get off on the side that is not near the footpath. If you do you might get run over.

RAYMOND, 7

Safety First

When you cross the road always look to the right and to the left. When there are no lights, cross where the lines are and you will be safe.

ANTONY, 7

Safety

When you want to get off a bus or a train you must wait until it has stopped. You must not jump off the bus when it is going because if there is a car coming you might get run over. Before you cross a road, you must look to the right, and look to the left and look to the right again.

CATHERINE, 7

The Policeman

Police help us in every way. The policeman helps by directing the traffic and he helps us when we are lost and when we fall off a cliff or when we are in trouble.

RAYMOND, 7

The Hospital

At the hospital the doctor and nurse help to make people better. Some doctors come to schools to see how well the children are. On Thursday we saw it all on TV. A doctor went to a school and he saw very healthy children.

THERESE, 7

Foot Doctors

Foot doctors are very smart because when Mandy was not skipping, the foot doctor put her in the hospital and cured her.

PATRICIA, 7

Doctors

Doctors are your friends. They will make you well. One day the doctor will come to your home or to your school. If you are sick he will make you better. He will give you medicine. He has to check you first of all. Then you must ask for your medicine every day.

ANTON, 7

Doctors and Nurses

Almost everywhere there are doctors and nurses. Each doctor has to know how every part of you works. If he does not, then how can he tell what's wrong with you?

MARK R., 7

The Accident

One day I had an accident. My mother called the ambulance because I had a big piece of glass in my leg. The doctor came and took the glass out and then I felt better.

HELLIO, 7

Each year the City of Sydney Health Officer visits our school to lecture and show films on hygiene and health to all classes, and also to inform children about the Anti-litter Campaign. This correlates with our television health and hygiene lessons, and our class themes on these topics. This year after the hygiene film we were treated to Walt Disney's *Litterbug*, which the children thoroughly enjoyed. They not only wrote on this subject but also painted anti-litter posters which were awarded prizes and displayed in the Sydney Town Hall. I will first quote from the children's writing on health. Raymond, who painted the outstanding posters, once more sets out his ideas in a clear and matter-of-fact way.

Be Healthy

If you are not healthy you should get healthy. If you want to do that, wash your hands before handling food and clean your teeth after eating. Clean your teeth at night too. and when you finish, have a bath. Open windows so that you can have fresh air, and eat your vegetables.

RAYMOND, 7

Health

Keep yourself clean and healthy. Before you eat you must always wash your hands. You will get germs if you don't wash them. So remember, don't ever eat before you wash your hands.

MARY, 8

Be Healthy

You should clean your teeth every day and wash your face and hands before you eat, and before you go to school. You should kill all insects with a spray. They spread diseases. You should keep your school clean too.

BARRY, 7

Healthy People

Healthy people are clean people because they wash their hands and their bodies all over with soap. They keep their houses tidy and kill all germs.

THERESE, 7

Flies

Flies carry germs. If you see a fly you must kill it with a fly-spray. Flies come into houses. They come through little holes.

MICHAEL L., 7

93

Soap

You must always clean yourself with soap, because you don't want to go to school with a dirty face. You must always be clean.

JULIANNE, 7

About Health

I clean my teeth every night and morning and I brush my hair. I have a shower every day to keep my body clean.

PATRICIA, 7

Be Clean

When you see a fly you must kill it or you will have germs in your house and you will get sick. You must wash your hands before you eat, too.

MARK A., 8

Health

You must brush your teeth after every meal because every meal leaves food behind. You must brush your hair too.

MARK R., 7

Health

You must always clean your teeth after every meal and you must wash your hands in hot water before you eat your meals. If you see a paper or something on the ground, pick it up and put it straight into the garbage bin and put the lid on.

CATHERINE, 7

Untidy People

People must not be dirty or they will be sick and will have to go to hospital. Some insects spread germs. They are flies, mosquitoes, and cockroaches. There are more. When you come out of hospital you can go back to school.

MICHAEL LO., 6

THE ANTI-LITTER CAMPAIGN

The Litterbug

I am not a fireman. I am not a policeman, but I am a bad litterbug. A litterbug throws papers on the road. It is not good for Sydney because we cannot pick them all up.

TIMOTHY, 7

Litter

Do not throw your papers around. You will make rubbish. Put papers in the right place. Do not throw them around.

CARMELLA, 8

Untidy People

Litterbug, why do you throw your rubbish away? You must put it in a rubbish tin. You must not throw it on the ground.

GRANT, 7

Papers

Don't throw papers. The sweeper-man comes to pick the papers up. Every day the sweeper-man picks up papers and he never gets any work done.

Sharon, 7

Litterbug

Litterbug, litterbug,
why are you untidy?
You throw your things all over the street.

Glen, 7

Paper

If you see any paper on the floor pick it up. As you know there are many men that always have to pick the papers up but they can't because there are too many papers in Sydney.

Mary, 8

Litterbug

Litterbug, litterbug, shame on you, throwing papers in the street. (Litter is paper and rubbish.)

Carmen, 7

Litterbug

Don't throw all around
papers on the ground.
Papers thrown,
papers blown,
all lie on the ground.

Mark R., 7

Litterbug

I was dropping papers in the street. I was carried away. I found out that I was in hospital. I had a big crawly litterbug on my back. They got it off and then life was worth living again.

Michael, 7

When Marianne had finished her story, I sent her to her place to write a verse. This was an experiment on my part to see what she would produce in a given time. I was quite amazed when she was back at my side in less than five minutes with this:

Don't drop papers for you know
the wind will come and it will blow.
It will blow your papers high away,
and your papers will be on the street today.

95

In the Prevention of Bushfires Campaign, children needed no prompting. They responded to school lessons and television programmes on what is, to so many in this country, a painful topic. These verses are uttered from the hearts of true little Australians.

Bush Fire

Crackling,
the fire starts,
It stretches over fields.
It pushes over trees
and burns down houses.
It burns grass and eats the wheat away.

MICHAEL LE., 7

Bush Fire

What's that glowing thing?
It's crackling and crawling
stretching and roaring.
It's coming nearer and nearer.
It's a fire!
Help! Help!

KIM, 7

Bush Fire

Busy fire brightly burning
golden sparks
jump out.
Glowing crackling
he is hungry.
Chasing sparks
spreading fire.
Leaping. Dancing.
That's a golden bush fire.

THERESE, 7

Bush Fire

Fire, fire, spitting up in flames.
Fire, fire, burning all the trees
You will burn nearly everything.

TIMOTHY, 7

Bush Fire

Fire! Fire!
Stretching out like hands.
Smoky, misty,
dusty, leaping,
stretching out like hands.

PATRICIA, 7

96

Raymond with his originality of thought and flair for English has created a character for his bush fire—Old Bush Tom Cat. He cleverly sustains his metaphor:

Bush Fire

Who's that coming down the track?
Why, it's Old Bush Tom Cat.
Hear him hissing.
—'Help!'
as they run out,
'Fire!'—
He spreads his feet far.
That's Old Tom Cat.
He's hungry now.
He's chasing.
He's jumping.
He's leaping.
That's Old Tom Cat!

RAYMOND, 7

7

We listen and dance

I am twirling around to the music,
I am swifting around and around.
The music makes me feel like doing ballet . . .
BRETT, 7

IN CHAPTER 1, the musical appreciation lesson was discussed as being a valuable aid to vocabulary extension. Not only does it give us more 'words for our work' but it provides a most fertile field for creative writing. Indeed it is true to say that music is indispensable in the education of children.

Why is this so?

Having worked with children and noted their reactions, I would say that music is an impelling force empowered to affect mind and heart and even to set the whole body moving in response to its rhythm. So we see heads nodding, arms beating time, bodies swaying and feet creating a spontaneous dance.

This individual outpouring of the child's self, his aspirations, thoughts, and feelings, through the medium of a chosen art form, is true creativity. Children who can evolve their own dance should be encouraged to find words to express themselves both orally and in writing. If they are to compose with a natural flow, it is important that the teacher receive and acknowledge their efforts, responding with due understanding and acceptance. At the same time she should provide them with unlimited opportunities for practice, because this is the most necessary condition for success. On their part, children need to feel that their efforts to reveal themselves will be accepted and respected.

From time to time there occurs in every classroom an occasion for spontaneous creativity. It happens of itself, without preparation or premeditation and is as thrilling as it is refreshing. It is quite unrehearsed and unexpected, but is totally satisfying in its aesthetic merits. One such occasion involving the use of music comes to my mind.

I clearly remember the day when my seven-year-olds were completing their rhythmic paintings to the delightfully gay music of Ibert's *Little White Donkey*. I became so engrossed in the children's response that I failed to notice that the recording had come to an end. Before I could adjust the tape-recorder a new and very different tune began. It was a bright piping melody with an irresistible lilt. No sooner had it begun than the children's faces lit up, brushes fell from their hands and they began to dance, springing nimbly on their toes, pirouetting, waltzing and swaying in the lightest and most natural movements I had ever seen.

There was not one still child in my class. Quite effortlessly, they interpreted the delicate parts of the music as a solo dance, and then swung into twos and threes as the heavier music impelled them to vary their response. As the rhythm slowed down and a pause warned them of a change in dynamics, the groups twirled apart for individual interpretation and then came together again to finish in a variety of graceful and picturesque group poses. This experience was a revelation to me of the power of music over the child's spontaneous expression. I felt that it was so fully creative that I could not trespass by asking the children to try to put it into words . . . What was this music that had played the Pied Piper to my class? It was one of the loveliest extracts I have ever used with children: the *Petite Ballerina* from Ballet Suite No 1 by Dmitri Shostakovitch.

Our children are always encouraged to weave their own stories around the music being studied. In order to develop in them the art of listening, we stipulate that the details of the music must be featured as incidents in the story and that the ideas must be original and true to the character and atmosphere of the extract.

In February, we began a study of *The Viennese Musical Clock* from the 'Háry Janós Suite' by Kódaly. Children wrote their own version of the vivid music.

Viennese Musical Clock
The bells are ringing. I saw a clock and every time it struck, toy soldiers came out. Then they started marching around the clock. It was so lovely that it made me cry.

MARY, 8

The Viennese Musical Clock
The soldiers march all around the clock slowly because there are lots of soldiers all around the clock.

CHRISTINA, 7

The Viennese Music
There was a man called Kodaly in Vienna. He went to a ball. He saw beautiful things but he thought the clock was the loveliest. When he went home he wrote music. He called it the 'Viennese Musical Clock'.

ANNE, 7

99

The Musical Clock

Can you hear the church bells big and loud? Every time the hour struck, little soldiers marched around the clock.

MICHAEL L., 7

The Viennese Clock

One night people went out dancing. When they were dancing the clock struck and all the toy soldiers came marching around the clock. Then after that the bells began to ring. 'Ding! Dong!' went the bells as the people went home.

MATTHEW, 7

Asked why they liked this music, children wrote:

I like the Viennese Musical Clock because it is so musical. It is gay and happy music and it is bright.

STEPHEN, 7

Kodaly wrote the Viennese Musical Clock and I like it because I can march to it, I can act to it, I can listen to it, and I can move to it.

PETER, 7

The composer of the Viennese Musical Clock is Kodaly. I like it because it tells a story about the soldiers having a parade. I can march to the music and it makes me feel as though I am a soldier too.

MICHAEL L., 7

The class next made a study of *The Little White Donkey* by the French composer, Jacques Ibert. Notice how the orchestration is interpreted by the children in a variety of ways.

A Donkey

There was a man who had a donkey. He set out on a journey. He was singing a merry tune when the donkey got a fright. He kicked up his legs but then went on his way.

ANNE, 7

The Donkey

Once there was a man riding a donkey and he was going slowly. There was a snake on the path and he was frightened. The snake poked out his tongue and then he went away. The donkey galloped along the road going, 'Ee-or! Ee-or!'

CHERYL, 7

The Donkey

There was once a little donkey and his master was a kind man. He was going to town so that he could seek his fortune. Along the way a rabbit ran in front of the little donkey and he started to run.

PETA, 7

Donkey

Once there was a man and he was going to town. His donkey saw a guinea pig and it jumped on a stone.

STEPHEN, 7

The Little White Donkey

It was spring and a little white donkey was in a field. He was hungry. The man on his back was whistling a tune. The donkey got a fright when a snake crossed his path.

PETER, 7

White Donkey

I like the little white donkey because it shows me calm rivers and peaceful hills. It tells me about a home where you love best. It shows that you can't work every minute. You need a rest.

MATTHEW, 7

(This is a deep philosophy for a child of seven to draw from a study of a musical selection.)

In their appreciation of *The Little White Donkey*, the class became very interested in the life of Jacques Ibert. Here are some of their versions:

The Boy Who Wanted to be an Actor

The boy, Jacques Ibert, was born in Paris. He wanted to be an actor and play the piano too. His father did not like him playing the piano so he learnt it secretly and then his father found out. He was sad because he wanted his son to be a shopkeeper. At last his father sent him to a school so that he could learn to play the piano well.

ANTON, 7

(Anton's own father is a shopkeeper. It is interesting to note that he adapted this idea from the word *businessman* in the original script.)

Jacques Ibert

Once there was a boy called Jacques Ibert. He wanted to learn to play the piano but his father did not want him to. So he played it secretly and his father was sorry for himself. Then his father took him to a good piano school. After a while, Jacques wanted to be an actor instead and he left the music school and forgot about music. At last he went back to his music and he caught up with the others. Then he wrote 'The Little White Donkey'.

MATTHEW, 7

Jacques Ibert

Jacques Ibert was born in Paris. His father wanted him to be a business man. But Jacques played the piano privately. Then his father knew that

101

he was playing the piano so he took him to a special school. Then Jacques learned how to be an actor for a little while. He went back to play the piano and caught up with the rest of the class. He wrote music about the little white donkey. Then his father said, 'I am sorry I stopped him from playing the piano.'

MARY, 7

A special television performance of the ballet *Giselle* for schools was a source of great enjoyment for our children. They were totally absorbed in this beautiful production with its appealing story in movement. When it was over, they were keen to list the vocabulary they wanted to use in writing about it. I was especially interested in the response of a slow-learning boy who had experienced great difficulty in reading and writing. Neither of his parents spoke English and the boy was withdrawn and had progressed very slowly. But this ballet session seemed to fire his imagination and unlock something within him. Of all the children in my class, only he wrote of the Prince. Notice the rhythmic flow of the lines, and the balance of the whole composition. The second sentence would be creditable for a post-primary pupil. I observed him at work and am certain that the composition was entirely his own.

The Ballet
The man was floating like a space-man. He was the most beautiful one in the whole world of all those people He tip-toes, he twists, and does movements too. He likes dancing all the time, and looks as if he is in space.

CHARLES, 8

Christine's poem has definite waltz rhythm befitting the theme:

The Ballet
Dancing girl,
dancing girl,
twisting and twirling,
you are so beautiful,
gently you go.
You spin so softly
and glide like a bird.

CHRISTINE, 7

The Ballet
Giselle felt like dancing. She told herself a story and then danced it with the Prince. She had point-shoes.

YOLANDA, 7

Ballet

Sway, sway,
swaying around,
you move fast
and sway fast.
Move around!
Don't stay in one place.
Move around!

KAREN, 6

The Ballerina

The ballerina twirled as hard as she could. I wish I was a ballerina so
that I could twirl as hard as I could.

ANTON, 7

Ballet

'See me!' said Giselle, 'I am telling a story with my movements.' Then the
Prince came and knocked on the door. Nobody answered. Then he
knocked again and Giselle came out. But the Prince went to hide, and
when Giselle came back he was gone, and out she danced. When she
knew that he was a prince, she was upset. Then she died because her
heart was broken.

VIVIANNA, 7

Giselle

I twist, I twirl, I spring.
I go up on my tip-toes and fly through the air.
I glide like a butterfly, high in the sky.

PETA, 7

Giselle

She springs like a spring,
she floats like the air,
she darts like a spear
flying through the air.

MICHAEL L., 7

Ballet

Tip-toe! Tip-toe!
go and spring and dance!
You float and spin.
and swing and sway and twirl.
Your shoes are pointy and sharp
and you dart like a spark.
You are very quiet when you dance.

MATTHEW, 7

103

Giselle

Giselle is a ballet dancer swaying her hands.
'Tip-toe', go her feet, darting and darting.
Her shoes are point-shoes.
She is lovely and calm.
It is beautiful dancing with the Prince.
It is good to twist and twirl like a spinning top.

NICHOLAS, 7

Ballet

She springs across.
She's spinning and spinning.
She is so gentle.
She dances so softly
that you could not hear her.
She is moving fast.
'Tip-toe, tip-toe.'

ROBERT, 7

Ballet Shoes

'Tip-toe, tip-toe,' goes Giselle,
her shoes so nicely tip-toe.
She feels so calm.
How soft her shoes are,
how light they are too.

KAREN, 6

Giselle

Tip-toe! Tip-toe!
Here she goes.
She twists and twirls.
She dances very softly
with her little pointy shoes.
She is flying like a robin.
Giselle doesn't make a sound.

MARY, 7

A boy who is learning to speak English wrote:

Ballerina

It was a gentle bright movement.
It danced around and around.

LUIGI, 7

The Ballerina

'Sway, little ballerina,
sway all night
in the moonlight.
You have a coloured dress,
pink, yellow, and orange.'

CATHERINE, 7

104

▲The idea of making a mosaic of our own seemed to grow of itself. Therese and Antony paste coloured paper 'tiles' in place while Anton replenishes the supply.

▼These children really appreciated the look of a beautiful page, well-lettered and aptly illustrated. Michael Le., and Mary, writing in Italic style with their fountain pens. Mary, a left-handed child, is using a special nib.

▲Children enjoy the moving experience of being literally in the midst of organ music. A Group of Grade 2 children write their impressions of the music.

▶Social Studies is fun! Michael Le. enjoys playing a native drum from Bundi, New Guinea, while Robert and Michael Lo., look on.

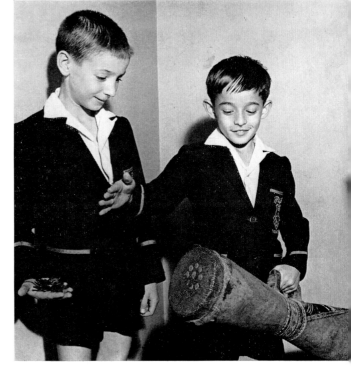

▼Musical Appreciation lessons are always popular with Grade 2 children. In our study of stringed instruments, Therese examines a violin.

▲ In their study of New Guinea, Patricia and Marianne are fascinated by a magnificent specimen of a Bird of Paradise.

◀ A close relationship between the arts is maintained in the Infant School. Raymond's beautiful painting of a stained-glass Crucifixion Window is matched by his well-written description. Silvana and Carmen paint fanciful animal-models about which they will write.

▲Advent brings with it the Advent Wreath Ceremony and the longing for the coming of the Saviour. Carmella lights the first candle.

▼In Advent, Christmas Cribs are made for every child's home. Yolande and Mark A. are absorbed in their task of setting up a crib.

The Children's Symphony, third movement, by the American composer Harl McDonald, was selected for our next musical experience. It is a clever medley of well-known tunes, and in this extract *Jingle Bells* and *The Farmer in the Dell* are featured. Our children were set the task of weaving the two tunes into one connected story. It is interesting to see how cleverly they have done this.

The Music

It looks as if the horses are out after the fox, and then the men blow the bugle right near the dogs. Then the horses start running so fast, and the men blow the bugle about ten miles away from the dogs. It starts to snow then, so they put a jingle-bell on their sleigh and start playing 'Jingle-bells', and the horses go along dancing.

YOLANDA, 7

(I was impressed by the way this child was conscious of the echo in the music and devised a way of using it in her story.)

The Hunt

Once there was a farmer in his field.
He heard a hunting horn,
and down the hill came hunting dogs, and
then the huntsmen,
at the front of all, a fox.

ANNE, 7

The Farmer in the Dell

The children were travelling along and the horses were too. The horses were making a noise too, and then came Rudolf. They saw Rudolf. He came with them too.

KAREN, 6

Playing

Five children were playing and singing,
'The Farmer in the Dell'.
Then the bell rang, and they all started to sing,
'Jingle Bells, Jingle Bells!'

SILVANNA, 7

Hunting

One day these men went hunting with bloodhounds. A man blew a bugle and the horses started running. After they stopped, the snow started to come down.

PETER, 7

Christmas and the Farmer in the Dell

Once there were men riding horses and they jumped over logs and they rode very fast. A man blew a french horn, and soon they stopped and rested. Soon it began to snow and the men went home.

MATTHEW, 7

The Farmer

There was once a farmer. He was hunting for a fox with his dogs. He stopped by a tree and had a rest. Then it was snowing. They went home and had tea. Then the bells rang and Father Christmas came to give the children toys.

GRANT, 7

The Farmer in the Dell

The children were hunting and singing,
'The Farmer in the Dell',
and then went the bells,
'Jingle-bells, Jingle-bells!'

ANTON, 7

The Hunting

One day there were horses and men, and they had a race. The men blew the bugles and the horses started running. After they stopped, the snow began to come down.

ROBERT, 7

Hunting

The men went hunting one day, and a man blew a bugle. In the distance, there was an echo of it. Then all of a sudden, the horses just dropped down and started to drink water. On the way back, it began to snow.

MICHAEL L., 7

The Farmer's Horses

The children went for a ride on the farmer's horses. They were happy on the horses. Then they had a rest behind the trees and began to sing, 'Jingle-bells, Jingle-bells!'

CARMEN, 7

A study of movement with and without music evoked some original ideas from the children:

Movement

Movement is a good thing to do. You can make curly movements, skipping movements and jumping ones too. When you do movement with other children you can make a pattern together. It could be a smooth pattern or some other kind.

MARY, 7

Movement

I can do all kinds of movements.
With my feet, I can dance, and
when I dance I can move my shoulders and
my body too.

CARMEN, 7

Movement

Movement is good. You can do all sorts of things with it. You can make patterns in fives. I like smooth and gentle patterns.

SILVANNA, 7

Movement

Movement takes you everywhere. If you want to make a dance you use movement, but it is easier to dance if you have music.

STEPHEN, 7

Movement

I stretch myself out like a mat.
I sway to and fro, to and fro.
I twist and turn and curl like a flower.

CHERYL, 7

Movement

Movement is a happy thing. You could tumble or tap your toe on the ground. You can do everything with movement.

NICHOLAS, 7

Movement

I think movement is a good thing because you could do very many things with it. You could run, jump and skip. God created movement. We wouldn't be alive if there was no movement. We need to run and to eat all kinds of good things. God made movement because he loves us very much.

MATTHEW, 7

One day in October my class climbed to the organ-gallery to learn about the organ. Never was there a more appreciative audience. After the mechanics of the instrument had been explained by our organist, children enjoyed the moving experience of being literally in the midst of organ music. My posting-box, where they are free to put their spontaneous writing at any time, was filled with their reactions.

The Organ

Hush goes the organ, soft and smooth
or as loud as a bear
or as soft as a gentle piece of hair;
and when it's very loud,
it's like a bear
that just touched the ground.

MARIANNE, 7

The Organ

The sounds of the organ are elegant and beautiful. It goes softly and loudly. The organ has pedals and stops. When it is soft, it sounds like an elf and it gets softer. The piano is too loud for the church. The air that is pumped into the organ by electricity makes all the sounds.

MICHAEL LE., 7

107

The Organ

The organ plays very loudly and very softly. It has a beautiful sound. It plays by electricity, and if you don't turn the electricity on, you don't hear any sound.

ANTONY, 7

An Organ

You play smooth sounds, rough sounds, loud sounds and soft, you sound like an orchestra.

KIM, 7

The Organ

It's like an orchestra.
It has a cello in the stops,
and oh! loud noises it has too.
It roars like the sea and the wind too.

MARK R., 7

An Organ

Hush, is the organ playing?
It's a lovely sound like a harp in heaven.
It goes softly as a tear-drop falling down.

RAYMOND, 7

The Organ

The pipes of the organ are big. It has to be pumped or it will make no sound. In olden days two boys had to pump it. Now it is pumped by electricity.

ANTONY, 7

An Organ

The organ roars and roars. It goes loudly and softly. It belongs in the church with the other holy things, not staying here with the piano.

GLEN, 8

The Organ

The organ is like a melody. Can't you see and feel the wonderful smooth sound? Can't you feel it in your soul like an orchestra? Can't you feel the beautiful melody?

MARIANNE, 7

The Organ

It's lovely when you play the organ. It makes you happy. Sometimes it makes you feel like crying, or it makes you feel like having a new life.

MARY, 8

The Organ

I am twirling around to the music. I am swifting around and around. The music makes me feel like doing ballet. The pipes make me swift around because they have electricity in them. The loud music makes me feel about the jungle, and the low music makes me feel about me doing ballet.

BRETT, 7

108

The Organ

As I listen to the organ, I feel as if I am floating on water. It is brilliant the way the music plays. It is fantastic the way it is smooth and gentle, just like birds slooping slooping down.

BRETT, 7

The Organ

Down, down in the forest,
screaming birds and screeching sounds . . .
All at once I saw these two bright eyes
shining in the dark,
looking at me as if I were an enemy.

CHERYL, 7

Organ

I feel like an angel in a concert
with St. Stephen, the composer.

STEPHEN, 7

The Organ

The organ is like a huge piano.
Before it starts, it is pumped with air.
But still it does not work.
You have to pull out a stop,
and then a huge voice covers the whole church,
and I hear an echo.

JOHN, 7

8

The world of story books

'He had a world of his own . . .'
RAYMOND, 7

THE IMPORTANCE OF STORIES in giving children a
rich vocabulary and a good English style has been discussed in
Chapter 1. Words in Colour has already played its part in preparing
children to benefit from literature. By exercising the dynamic
imagery of their minds, it has served to build up their judgment not
only to choose the right sign in spelling but also to be able to discriminate and decide for themselves what is correct and desirable
in the form and style of their writing. The whole tenor of the Words
in Colour course has been to encourage children's inventiveness and
originality and to give them the power to manipulate words into
meaningful patterns. It is true that there is no beaten track leading
to creativity, nor is there one to the mastery of Words in Colour,
but both activities may go hand in hand as an expression of in-
dividuality. Each child acts on the materials in a different way and
every class proceeds at a different rate. At the same time each pupil
contributes gifts of his own and absorbs gifts from others. Thus a
power over words and an understanding of acceptable forms of
English are gained, and with these the ability for a deep appreciation
of all that is beautiful in literature.

It is not desirable, however, that stories be always subjected to
intensive language analysis. They are, above all, works of art
which convey us into their own world. Let children enjoy the story
as a whole, just as they enjoy music; for they listen to a melody
until the last note dies away, and a moment of silence ensues. This
is the moment when one realises that there is a spiritual and aesthetic
value in the arts, a personal communication that does not bear the
rude clatter of conversation. For this reason all our stories have
not given rise to free creative writing but they have done far more

for our children, by enriching their minds and unconsciously heightening the standard of their English.

At times, however, when creative writing is to be assigned, a well-chosen story often gives the desired impetus. Usually a discussion should precede the actual writing. In this way the teacher raises the level of awareness in children, helping them to see, hear, feel, taste, or touch, so that they will be at home in the subject and know it intimately. The superficial child who has but a few ideas and only a smattering of knowledge, can be transformed into the child who is aware and who writes what he feels because he has lived in his subject and belongs. The discussion will therefore provide some kind of outline which will help children to colour their topic with personal ideas and feelings. They must have liberty, too, to draw from the fathomless depths of their imagination. Moreover, they need the security of working with an appreciative and understanding guide who will open now one door, now another, taking great care never to lock any but to keep on opening avenues which help children to write, in poetry or prose, to experiment with words, and thus to express themselves about whatever is near or dear to them.

Nor will the teacher expect a perfectly written first copy any more than she herself would produce an important script without dashing off ideas, scrapping this part and that, trying again, and finally arriving at what she wanted to say, as she knows it should be said. If she insists rigidly on the perfect setting out of a first copy then she will find a matching tightness of expression and a lack of buoyancy and gaiety.

What of the children's spelling in the rough draft? The use of colourful expressions which carry them away in the exuberance of happy thought may not always pair with meticulous attention to faultless spelling. The writing of English is an art to be acquired gradually. No doubt sincere and thoughtful writing with some spelling errors is to be preferred to perfectly spelt stereotyped work without life or meaning. I usually find that the child who does the first type of writing is so full of ideas that he is not always conscious of spelling correctly. However, should I query the offending word it is quite quickly corrected.

If the child has never seen the word and really cannot spell it, then we happily add it to our list of words to be studied at spelling time. The treatment is simple. If the word is not on the word charts, we look at it written on the chalkboard. Children read it. The component signs are then discovered on the Fidel. The word is then covered. Children can now write it unaided and, as a general rule, know it. To make sure that the erring ones are quite at home with it I test them again in varied ways; e.g., asking the child to find it on the Fidel (Visual Dictation I) or asking him to write it or, again, asking him to point out certain signs within the word, especially those connected with his initial error. Thus, in Stage 4, spelling lists are compiled from the mistakes children make in their free creative writing and spelling errors are easily eradicated. Should some children continue to make errors in words known by the rest of the class, the treatment is carried out again with a small group or even with a single child.

Finally, in creative writing, the child should be free to write on any aspect of the topic in hand because he can only write convincingly on something that is vital to himself.

This year each of our books and stories has carried us into another world, but the spell and wonder that remained have not always been tangible enough to be translated into words. Some children, however, have chosen to write, and their ideas reveal the depth of their understanding.

One story that captured children's imaginations was an original tale about a friendly witch. It was told in a very dramatic style, but in the re-telling children fabricated their own details and thus made the story their own.

The Friendly Witch

Once upon a time there was a witch. She was friendly and she had a magic paint-brush. The paint-brush would do anything she said. It just so happened that the King and Queen were coming next afternoon. Everyone was busy except one person, one naughty little elf . . .

SHARON, 7

Snoozy

Snoozy was a little elf. He was too lazy to move. Once he took a brush and set it to work. He could not make it stop, but the witch told it to stop and it did. Then the Queen and King arrived and they had a party.

MARK A., 8

The Friendly Witch

Once upon a time there was this old lady. She was a witch and she had a magic paint-brush. She said the magic words: 'Ager, Mazger, Zama, Maxu, paint the chimney brown and the ceiling red.' Now this lazy elf did not do any work. He went into the witch's house and took the paint-brush and ran home. He tried to say the magic words. 'I know', said the elf, 'Ager, Mazger, Zama, Mazu! Paint the door red and the chimney brown. 'Ha! ha! ha!' said he, 'the children will be surprised when they hear this.'

Soon the elf said, 'Now you can stop', but oh the brush did not stop although it knew how to take care of itself . . .

MARY, 8

The Friendly Witch

There was once a bad witch who changed a good fairy into a witch. Her wand was changed into a magic paint-brush. One day she went to the forest. She said the magic words, 'Spinkety, Spankity, spunkety spoo, you may paint the leaves green, and the branches gold, too!'

At that time a little elf was there, standing behind the trees. One day the fairy postman delivered a letter. There was a letter for everyone. They were all there except lazy old Snoozy the elf. The letter said that the King and Queen were coming to visit them. His friends came to tell Snoozy. He was in bed. His friends went with a bang on the door. The one day the friendly witch went out and Snoozy stole her brush. When he got back home his friends came and said, 'You had better finish your work', Snoozy said the magic words. The brush began to paint. It painted his room and door a fine green. When it was finished Snoozy said 'Stop', but it didn't stop. Just then the fairy who owned it came. She said 'Stop' and it did. She forgave him. At that moment she became a fairy again, because she had been kind.

MARIANNE, 7

After the story of the *Red Balloon* children were caught in a world of imagination and showed more inclination to write rhythmic lines than prose.

The Balloons

Red balloons, red balloons,
floating in the skies
above us,
flying flying
in the skies
all day long.

GLEN, 7

The Red Balloon

I saw a balloon
race past my eyes
high in the skies
of Paris.
There high in the skies
floats the red balloon.

RAYMOND, 7

The Balloons

Balloons, balloons,
filling the streets of Paris.
From the East and the West
you come,
from the South and the North too
filling the streets of Paris.

KIM, 7

113

The Red Balloon

Balloon, balloon,
passing by
with red and golden colours.
Red balloon flying high,
floating on the air.
Up with aeroplanes and birds
and with the other balloons,
with red and green balloons.

MICHAEL LE., 7

The Balloon

Look, look
I see a balloon.
A balloon, a balloon,
high in the sky.
I'm going to catch it
I'm going, going
to catch it.
Oh, yes I am!
I've never had a balloon before.

MARY, 7

The Balloon

If I had a red balloon I would teach it to obey me. I would say 'Come to me' and it would come sometimes. When I went to church I would tell it to wait and it would.

SHARON, 7

The Balloon

I'd like to have a balloon that is all mine. I'd teach it all the things I want it to do. Oh I wish I had a balloon.

MARY, 7

In Chapter 2, I cited the treatment of the gospel story of the Cure of the Blind Man. Almost every child chose to write on this topic and their work reveals a pleasing sensitivity. Perhaps the most outstanding contribution came from the pen of Hellio, our little Spanish boy, who is mastering English so well.

The Blind Man

If I was blind I would see pitch-black. I could smell and touch and feel. Then Our Lord, the Light of the World, would come to me. He would spit on the ground and put mud on my eyes. Then I could see that everything was colourful. Thank you God for making me see. Amen.

HELLIO, 8

114

Blind

If you were blind you would see nothing but darkness. But you could hear, smell and touch things. You might feel gloomy. If Jesus made you see again you would see lots of colours. It would be as if you were asleep for a hundred years and just woke up and saw all the colours suddenly.

MARK A., 8

The Blind Man

He had a world of his own. He could feel. He could smell and hear to learn. He was blind. Then one day Our Lord cured him. Yes, Our Lord spat on the ground and made clay and put in on the blind man's eyes and he was cured.

RAYMOND, 7

About Darkness

When we close our eyes we may get gloomy. We can feel our nose and our face. We can touch, hear and also speak. When we smell a flower it seems like perfume. But when we can see we can look at flowers, boats and planes. We have to thank God for letting us see.

MICHAEL Le., 7

The Blind Man

The blind man can't see, because he was born blind. He is very sensitive and other people are sensitive too. When the man was cured he jumped around the place and said, 'I'm cured! I'm cured!'

JULIANNE, 7

The Blind Man

A blind man can't see but he can hear, think, eat and touch. We can see, but God wants to test him. Then one day Jesus spat on the ground and wiped clay on his eyes and said, 'Go, wash in the pool.' Then he could see. He was jumping up and down. He was singing out, 'I can see! I can see!'

THERESE, 7

The Blind Man

He may not see but he can feel, touch, and hear. He can smell. He can feel the water with his feet. He can easily taste things, too, but he can only see darkness. Then Jesus came down and told him to go and wash in a pool. How excited he was because it was the first time he had seen such bright things. Thank you God for letting me see. Amen.

MARY, 8

Early in November we considered the Parable of the Sower. Children grasped the hidden meaning at once and many wrote their observations.

The Sower
As the sower sows the seeds, the word of God
comes down.
Jesus saw a sower
planting seeds.
There were roses with thorns
that stuck into the seeds.

Mark A., 8

The Sower and the Seed
A man went sowing seeds. One went on hard ground. Another, the birds
took away. The heat shrivelled one. The thorns choked another. But one
was buried and it grew. The one that grew was God's love.

Michael Lo., 7

Word of God
A man went out
to sow some seeds
sow some seeds
sow some seeds,
and that man dropped some seeds
on the hard ground.
Some got choked
but others grew
like the People of God.

Timothy, 7

The Sower
The sower threw a seed on a piece of hard rock.
The plant got dried
and died.
The other seed
on the soft soil
grew and grew
until it had seeds
opening out.
That was God's word.
And all that wheat grew.

Michael Le., 7

Word of God
The sower sows the seeds
and only some are choked with weeds.
All the others have fallen down
into the deep ground.
The fresh and beautiful ones
are standing looking up
and praying to God
who made them all.

Mary, 8

The Sower

There was a sower
who was in the field.
He threw some seed on soil.
Then the thorns strangled the plant.
He threw some
on the good soil
and it grew into lovely wheat. Amen.

GLEN, 7

Sower

Once a sower
was sowing his wheat.
He found out
that the wheat was not growing
because it was on the stony road,
or the birds ate it.
But only one seed out of ninety
did grow in the right soil.

THERESE, 7

Not only did children enjoy writing about known stories but they also delighted in making up stories of their own. As early as June this year Antony brought me a paper which read:

Courageous Cat

Courageous Cat goes on many trips. Once he went to a scarey place. He saw a witch there but he did not know what it was. Courageous Cat saw the witch fly and he said to himself, 'If that could fly, can't I try?' The witch saw him and made him fly, and made him land right in front of her house. Courageous Cat went inside the house. Now when the witch comes back she is going to turn Courageous Cat into a prince. But he does not want that to happen so he jumps out of the window.

Antony wrote his second story in this series about a week later.

Courageous Cat goes to the Moon

Courageous Cat is a brave cat. Today he is going to the moon but before he goes there he does want to know if there are any creatures living on the moon.
'Courageous Cat, I am afraid that nobody can tell us that except the people who have been there.'
When Courageous Cat arrives on the moon he will see lava in those deep holes. He will see mountains, too.
'Courageous Cat, I am afraid you will have to be locked in a cage in the rocket ship. You are a wonderful cat.'

The third example of Antony's story-writing was:

The Haunted Castle

Courageous Cat is going to a castle today with his partner, Mickey Mouse. Courageous Cat told Mickey Mouse that the castle was haunted and it was. When they got to the door there was a big yell. Courageous Cat said to Mickey Mouse, 'I told you this castle was haunted.' Mickey Mouse said, 'There are no such things as ghosts.' Then they went inside the castle. When they got halfway through it they heard the yell again. Courageous Cat said, 'Let's get out of here!' He was so scared that he jumped right out of his skin.

The one that yelled was a little boy who lived in Courageous Cat's house, and when they saw each other they both fainted.

Michael L. commenced his adventure of Yogi Bear and Boo-Boo towards the end of second term. Here is one of the episodes:

One Summer's morning in Jellystone National Park, Yogi Bear was walking with Boo-Boo. Boo-Boo said, 'Look, there is a basket on that table with some chicken and meat and milk in it.'

Yogi Bear replied, 'What are we waiting for?' They both went to it but it was not full of food—there was a dog inside and he chased them all over the park. So the two bears did not do that again.

When they got home Boo-Boo said to Yogi Bear, 'It was a long day today.'

Yogi said, 'Why don't we have a nap?'

So they did.

9

A child's day

'Good day dear God
I will sing to you
tomorrow and today.'
CARMELLA, 8

IF FREE CREATIVE WRITING is to flourish amongst
our pupils, we should give them plenty of encouragement and
incentive to write continually. A posting box is a necessity in the
classroom so that daily jottings of incidental happenings and the
flashes of insight that strike the child may not be lost but may reach
the teacher easily and informally.

I must confess that I go to my posting box every evening feeling
like a diver in sight of pearls. I realise that not all the work, nor
even half of it, will be impeccable; but I prize every piece of sincere
writing as a mirror of the child's mind and I see beneath its rough
shell the lustrous pearl of living thought.

Sometimes, too, the posting box becomes a forum, as when a note
in a childish hand asked if she could be moved from a neighbour who
annoyed her in some way. Another child, aware of this posted
request, wrote in: 'Please Sister, don't move me from Mary. She
is my best friend.' The friend also contributed, 'Sister, Sharon and I
work better when we are together.'

Whimsical little 'Please' and 'Thank you' notes, prayers and
wishes find their way into the posting box and the shy child is never
afraid to use it. All rough drafts of writing are posted for my checking
and work of quality is returned to children the next morning. These
children then pen their stories on blank foolscap paper and illustrate
them. They enjoy using the two-hole punch themselves and file the
pages into their own folios.

Some work requires discussion and I find that I can do this
satisfactorily only if the child is beside me. So while most children

119

are occupied penning their stories, I may take now this child, now that, to discuss quietly how this work may be improved.

I use the word *pen* deliberately. Traditional script-print done in pencil is unlovely because it lacks character and style. Therefore this year, in the month of August, I began experimenting with the italic handwriting. I sharpened to a chisel-point our thick-leaded pencils and we commenced work. The results were satisfying but not completely effective. Ink was necessary as the medium for expressing this particular hand and I could not imagine ink bottles in the infant school. The answer, obviously, was a chisel-nibbed fountain pen. Finding that such did exist, we purchased fountain pens in Term 3 and one bottle of black ink in a pretty tin filled with pen-wipe fabric.

We have not looked back since then and our days have been marked by a happy endeavour to improve our handwriting. These children really appreciated the look of a beautiful page, well lettered and aptly illustrated. Their parents were amazed. Leslie's proud father had him pen his 'Snail' story six times so that he could show it far and wide. Here again, Words in Colour is the provider because, by the concentrated nature of its course, it allows time for infant school children to pursue such a profitable art as this. Given another experimental year I would introduce italic writing earlier.

Thus it is that day by day we have triumphs to show. It is important that the class share in them and that the child who has composed a beautiful poem or story should read it to the others.

The following extracts from children's writing have all found their way to my posting box this year. They reveal details of a child's day, his loving worship and his wonder no less than his round of work and games, all coloured with the exuberance and enthusiasm of childhood.

God our Father

Good day dear God,
I will sing to you
tomorrow and today.
I will be good.
I will think of You
today and tomorrow
I will love You dear God,
tomorrow and today.

CARMELLA, 8

120

Bird's Songs

Sing little birds!
Sing,
Sing,
Sing to me.
Sing your morning song to me.

CARMEN, 7

Morning

I love to look out of my window
and see what weather it is
and take my dreams of night away.
I love to see
what exciting things there are.

MARY, 8

Birthdays

We each have a birthday
one day in the year.
Maybe in March, or April, or May.

MARK, 7

My Rose

I brought a rose to school to put on the altar. It was pink. Sister liked that rose because pink is her favourite colour. She put it on the altar and said it looked nice there.

BARRY, 7

My School Dictionary

I have a dictionary that is red. It has more than one hundred pages. It has four hundred. I got the dictionary for my birthday.

CLAUDIO, 7

Tree

Tree, you stand still.
You have branches.
You are nice to climb,
sometimes.

CARMELLA, 8

The First Time at School

When I was five I went to school. I didn't like it. I cried. When I was about six I got used to it, and now I like school.

ANTONY, 7

The Weather

At this time of the year we have fine weather. It is nice and warm. I like warm weather and I like the fresh wind to come up in the afternoon. I like to see the thunderstorm and the sky get dark and cloudy.

ROBERT, 7

God

God made the birds.
God made the ants.
The trees are tall.
The flowers are small.
The leaves are little and green.

HELLIO, 7

Seagull

I saw a seagull. Its leg was cut.
I took it home. My father fixed it up and then
the seagull ate some fish.

ANTONY, 7

Nests

We didn't have
one bird's nest
two
or three.
We had six,
in our poplar tree.

MARK R., 7

The Park

I go out on a wintry day. Guess where I'm going? Yes, I'm going to the park. The trees are bare and the birds are getting berries for their tea. There are so many interesting things in a park.

KIM, 7

Winter

It is cold because it is winter. It is very cold this time. Sometimes it rains in the night. The sun is further away. We sleep longer and the sky is darker too.

MICHAEL LO., 7

My Radio

I have a radio that is brown. It tells me the news. It tells me the names of the football players. One day it told me that Johnny Raper lost his points and isn't playing any more.

CLAUDIO, 7

My Football

My football is brown and green. I was Balmain and Gregory was St George. My score was twenty and Gregory's was nine. I was the winner. Everyone said 'Good on you!' I was their friend. Nearly everyone asked me to sign my autograph for them. The last man asked if he could play with me.

CLAUDIO, 7

Swimming

Swim, swim in the water.
I can swim fast and slowly,
so slowly that I can put my head right under
the water.

SILVANA V., 7

The Policeman

One day my mother said I could go for a walk but I got lost. Then I went around the streets looking for a policeman. I went down to a corner and around twice. Then I saw him, a big tall policeman. I went to him and said 'I am lost, please take me home.' And he did.

PATRICIA, 7

The Duck

One day we went out and we saw a little duck walking along the sand. I said to Daddy, 'There's a little duck.' Daddy said, 'I think he is lost. We will look after him for a month.' Then Daddy got the duck and brought him home with us.

MICHAEL L., 7

Air

Air goes softly by. It moves like soft green grass. It is really nothing we can see. But it is good for people to breathe and not to die.

CARMEN, 7

Spring

Spring is here. Look at the beautiful things
there are.
Look! Look! Look!
There are the wonderful bees.
They are gathering nectar and pollen too.

GLEN, 7

The Zoo

We went to the zoo on Sunday. We saw the monkeys and the giant tortoises. We had fun on the merry-go-round and the train. We saw lots of other things but I liked the train best because it went around four times and made a roaring sound.

SHARON, 7

A Flower

Whenever a flower grows there must be a root or it will die. First there are the roots, then the shoot. The bud comes next and then the flowers.

CATHERINE, 8

Skating

I can skate on the veranda but not on the concrete. Soon I will be able to skate everywhere.

MARK R., 7

After the story *Bambi's Children* had been enjoyed, Raymond wrote these appealing lines:

Spring

Birds, come!
I see spring is here.
For joy you do your nesting.
Bees and butterflies
come out!
Bees, come to get your honey.
Butterflies to live a new life.
Animals, come!
For I see the path of spring
waiting for you.
Oh, do come out
for Spring is here
When flowers grow.
Oh, do come out!

RAYMOND, 7

Springtime Thank You

Thank you God for the lovely world
and the trees and the bees.
Thank you God for everything
and even our voices that can sing.

MICHAEL L., 7

The Monster

On Monday I saw the strangest animal. It was a green-eyed dragon with thirteen tails. Mummy would not believe me. Then she saw it and said, 'Oh-h-h!'

MARK R., 7

The Monster

I went out in my yard and there was a big animal with eight eyes, two tails, eight spines, ten teeth, four heads with pink noses, and a big loud roar. He scared the daylights out of me.

MICHAEL L., 7

After we had seen the film *The Greatest Story Ever Told* children cast about for a different medium to express their thoughts and feelings. We had already discussed the Ravenna Mosaics as works of art, and the idea of making a mosaic of our own seemed to grow of itself. Claudio outlined the figures for a close-up scene of the Last Supper with Our Lord and four apostles. Coloured advertisements from the shiny papered magazines were cut into small 'titles' in box lids. Each lid held pieces of only one colour but literally dozens of shades and textures. Using a large coloured illustration of the

Ravenna Mosaics as our guide, the whole class participated in the work of pasting the bright paper effectively. Perhaps this was the most satisfying project we have ever done, and the result was so finished-looking that Michael L. said, 'Everyone will think that we bought it'. A few children chose to write about it.

Mosaic

Yellow, silver, gold,
Ravenna told
to make a mosaic.
Halo bright
with all its might
shines on the Virgin Mary
like a light.
That's the mosaic
of the Virgin Mary.

MARIANNE, 7

Mosaics

Ruby red
for Virgin's dress . . .
White pearl
for Virgin's pure face . . .
Emerald green
for Virgin's cloak . . .
Monks from churches
made the Mosaics,
bright as silver
glowing in the dark.

RAYMOND, 7

Mosaic

Diamond colours
and ruby red
makes a precious mosaic
of the Virgin Mary
with emerald rocks
and golden halo
over Mary Virgin's head.

MICHAEL LE., 8

The Snail

One day I walked out in the garden. I saw something moving. It had big horns and a strange face. It squirmed and squiggled. It was so small. I ran to see what my mother thought it was. She said it was a snail.

Visitors

Miss Campbell has been all over the world. She went by air. When she had been everywhere, she came to Australia on her way home. She saw Words in Colour at our school and she taught us some words used in Hawaii.

CLAUDIO, 7

The Weather

One day we went to the seaside. There were many boats to be seen. It was very hot when we first got there but in a little while the sea began to get rough. 'A hurricane is here,' said Dad. I asked, 'What is a hurricane Dad?' 'When the wind goes 75 miles and hour,' he said. 'Sometimes it can cause a lot of trouble.'

THERESE, 7

Kangaroo

Kangaroo
let us go
over the mountains.
Not so slow,
but so fast
that no one
can see us.
Fast, fast,
over the mountains,
fast.

MARIANNE, 7

Koala

Koala, koala, eating gum leaves all day long. The baby is drinking its mother's milk. When it is four months old it gets on its mother's back to see the world.

LESLIE, 7

Backbone

A fish has a backbone and also it has fins to help it to swim. That shows how great God is to make a wonderful backbone.

GLEN, 7

The Eye Doctor

Today I had to go the eye doctor so that he could test my eyes to see if I needed glasses. He told me that I had to have glasses. 'You will have the glasses today,' he said.

MICHAEL LE., 7

Long Ago

Long ago in a city lived a little lady. She was dressed in white and red. She had two babies. When they grew up she died and they cried.

CARMEN, 7

126

My Car

I have a car. It is red and white. I get the petrol at Ampol. I always get half a gallon. On Thursday I had a car race. I won a hundred points.

CLAUDIO, 7

A Wet Day

One day when it was raining Mum said that we could play in the house, me, my sister and a very rough boy. We were playing hide and seek. Suddenly the rough boy pushed me and I landed on Mum's best jar. Pam said, 'Let's mend it.' I said, 'Let *him* mend it.' Mum came in and looked very surprised. She said, 'Who broke my jar?' The boy said, 'I did, I pushed *her*.' Mum was pleased that he told the truth and smiled. He gave her some money for it but Mum was only glad he was sorry and she said, 'Have the money back'.

THERESE, 7

Cats

Some cats are white.
Some cats are brown.
They play in Mum's knitting wool
and get caught in it.
They have milk and meat
to drink and eat.
They are friendly
and I hope you like them
as much as I do.

SHARON, 7

Cats

They scratch
and scratch
with their paws.
They play with knitting wool
and sometimes get caught.

MARY, 8

The Cats

Some cats have stripes and some are plain. Some are black and white. We have a tom cat. His name is 'Mittens'. He likes meat but his favourite food is fish and a drink of milk.

KIM, 7

After morning recess one day in September, a beautiful pigeon flew on to the school steps outside our classroom. He stayed for so long pecking about there that we gradually emerged to watch him. Children's interest drove them closer and closer to the bird but it did not fly away. Instead, as Michael L. wrote later, 'every time somebody would step up, he would step up another step', to keep himself a comfortable distance from us.

Pigeons

Pigeons are lovely. They fly beautifully through the air. We saw a lovely pigeon on Friday. He was eating crumbs. We all had a look.

TIMOTHY, 7

The Pigeon

The pigeon has lovely colours on its neck, red, green and brown. Every time somebody would step up, he would step up another step. He was eating the crumbs up. We called him 'Tidy Boy'.

MICHAEL L., 7

The Pigeon

We had a pigeon at school on Friday. He was our Tidy Bird. He had bronze on his neck and he was tidying our stairs.

MARK R., 7

The Pigeon

The pigeon had a broken wing and his neck had silky colours. The colours were green and purple. It pecked at food as it hopped from step to step. I was looking at it and I said to myself, 'It is very interesting to look at'.

MICHAEL LE., 7

Pigeon

Pigeons are lovely. They have lovely colours around their necks. The colour is green. In the sun it shines. When we go into school the pigeon comes. It eats the little bits we drop.

CARMELLA, 7

Pigeon

The pigeon is tidy bird. Gaily he flies high in the sky. He has very nice colours around his neck. In our class we call him 'Tidy Boy'.

RAYMOND, 7

Pigeon

Pigeons have grey feathers and white underneath. Their neck is sort of gold in the sun. We call ours 'Tidy Boy'.

ANTONY, 7

The Litter-Pigeon

The litter-pigeon is a good pigeon to have. He cleans the city for you. He eats the scraps that lie around. He is a tidy pigeon.

CATHERINE, 7

The Pigeon

The little pigeon goes up the steps
clip clop he goes.
He looks around
he doesn't make another sound
all around he goes
'clip clop' he goes.

MARIANNE, 7

128

The Pigeon

One day there was a pigeon at school. The children told Sister. She said, 'Let's call him 'Tidy Boy' because he is tidying our steps.' After a while, at home time, the pigeon was finished.

CHRISTINA, 7

During October a local guild organised a children's art contest. The title set for illustration was 'The Street I Live In—People or Houses'. Since all children were keen to participate, I used the theme for intensive language treatment as well as for art, so that the one could complement the other. Among the stories and poems I selected was a short verse 'Do houses say "Hi" to you?' This captured the interest of the class immediately and added an atmosphere of make-believe and wonder to our study. It also triggered children to write as well as to paint imaginatively. Only one child was too matter-of-fact to admit of the possibility of houses talking.

The House

A house cannot talk. It is for someone to live in. Your family could live in the house.

YOLANDA, 7

Houses

"Hi!" said one house.
'Goodbye,' said another.
But only one house
didn't say a word.
All the other houses
were talking like mad.
That house had not talked
all day long.

TIMOTHY, 7

A House

Down the street stands the creepy shack. Every day I pass this creepy shack I feel sad for it. I wish they'd do it up.

RAYMOND, 7

Houses

My house is not too small and not too big. It has all the things that it should need. It's the perfect house for me.

MARY, 8

A Friendly House

Do houses say 'Hello' to you as you pass? It is like a dream. They are like people in disguise. Don't you hear houses talk to you?

MICHAEL LE., 7

129

Houses

Do houses say 'Hi!' to you?
Yes they do.
Some 'Boo' and scare you.
Some say 'How do you do?'
(Some houses are friendly
and some are not.)

KIM, 8

My House

My house is a little house.
It is a blue and red house.
It says 'Hello' when I come
and 'Goodbye' when I go.

CARMEN, 7

Houses

Do houses say 'Hi' to you
as you walk by?
Some houses say nothing
and some do.
I like to see the size of all the houses.

BARRY, 7

Houses

A house in my street
is talking.
I think it is saying
'Hi!' to me.
It is not old
but it is so lonely.
I like my street
and houses.
They all say 'Hi!' to me.

CARMELLA, 7

130

House

Little house, little house,
red, blue and white,
going up, going up
with lovely red tiles.
It must have a bathroom.
It must have a kitchen.
It must have a dining room
and a lovely bedroom too.
Little house, little house,
red, blue and white,
going up, going up,
with lovely red tiles.
It must have a garden.
It must have some trees.
It must have a statue
and a lovely fountain too.

CATHERINE, 8

Speaking Houses

When I walk past the houses
I hear them saying 'Hey!' and 'Hello!'
They say, 'Where are you going?'
I say, I'm going to school.'
Then I say, 'I'd better move on or else
I will be late for school.
Goodbye, I will see you this afternoon, house.'

SHARON, 7

Sharon's painting of her street was one of the most appealing and was awarded a Special Prize.

Marianne's picture was scrawly and unfinished compared with the others. At the last moment I decided to send it in because it was so full of the bustle of childish activity. It won first prize! I was interested to note that her writing was not about houses but about the games she played out of doors with her friends.

My Street

Run, run, run,
Come out and play.
It's very happy sunny day
so come out, come out and play.
Run down where the three roads meet
and your running feet
Rush down the street
to play with your friends all day.

MARIANNE, 7

Towards the end of October we had an interesting discussion on the subject of 'noises'. This gave rise to much spontaneous writing which was full or originality.

Noises

Noises are loud and soft,
They rattle and tattle and tittle.
They go all day,
on and on they go.

ANTONY, 7

Noises

Noises we hear everywhere.
I hear noises every day: piano noises,
TV noises, bird noises.
Everywhere and everyday
I hear noises.

RAYMOND, 7

Noises

'Boom! tap!' 'What's that?'
'It is the shop on wheels.'
'Clip clop' goes the horse as it passes by.
In the night I hear something go
'Oo-o-oh!' It must be an owl.

KIM, 7

Noises

Noises are loud, noises are soft,
noises hush by you.
When you're in the bush,
noises boo by you.
Hush, boo, hush, boo,
as noises pass by you.

MARIANNE 7

Noises

There are all kinds of noises,
loud, soft, big and small,
angry noises
and people talking
up and down the town,
and upon the top of the steps,
and even in beds.
But I will never know
where all these noises come from.
I wish I knew.

THERESE, 7

Noises

'Tip-tip' goes the typewriter.
'Bang-bang' goes the thunder.
'Lash-lash' goes the lightning.
All sorts of sounds there are today.

PATRICIA, 7

Sounds

Sounds, sounds, loud and soft,
I like you very much.
With a screech and a boo,
you screech at people
and at me too.

MARIANNE, 7

As a foundation for the following section of creative writing, I used my natural science programme, coupled with direct observations throughout the year which related to insect and animal life. In order to utilise this knowledge and channel it into literary expression, I used Rumer Godden's translation of *Prayers from the Ark* by Carmen Bernos de Gasztold for poetry appreciation. These prayers were intended to give the children ideas as well as enjoyment. The class was then asked to think out individual prayers which were to be true to the character and habits of whatever creature might be chosen. This proved to be a highly engrossing and satisfying task as the results indicate.

The Prayer of the Blue Fanny Butterfly

Dear God, you know that I only want camphor laurel trees.
You make them tall.
They have fine little brown leaves on them.
That is where I lay my eggs.   Amen.

ANNE, 7

The Prayer of the Bee

O God, thank you for making me beautiful.
Some people try to kill me but I get away.
I make a buzzing noise.
I look camouflaged on flowers.
O thank you God for making me camouflaged.   Amen.

PETER, 7

The Prayer of the Fish

Please, dear God, help me to swim,
and then I can have lots of rides on the waves,
and swim all over the sea,
and live happily.   Amen.

JOHN, 7

133

The Prayer of the Snake

Sss . . .! Ss . . .! listen! . . .
I am the snake . . . I creep . . .
O Lord, help me to creep and crawl
to catch my food.
'Sssssssss . . .' I say.   Amen.

PETA, 7

The Animals Prayer

I am a kangaroo.
I jump and jump.
I am grey.
God, why do they shoot me?   Amen.

BRETT, 7

The Prayer of the Possum

O God, I am a possum.
I go out at night to get my dinner,
and then in the morning I stay at home, asleep.   Amen.

NICHOLAS, 7

The Prayer of the Duck

O God, I have not any water.
Please, God, will you let it rain tomorrow,
so that I will have a lot of water.   Amen.

SILVANNA, 7

The Prayer of the Duck

O God, how beautiful and holy you are!
But look at me,
I am just a duck.   Amen.

ANNA, 7

The Prayer of the Koala

O God please help me because I eat slowly
and they make fun of me
and I am sad.   Amen.

CHRISTINE, 8

The Prayer of the Koala

Dear God, please make my gum tree high,
and make more leaves.   Amen.

NICHOLAS, 7

The Prayer of the Koala Bear

Dear God, how good you are!
Thank you for these trees.
I'm so happy to have my baby on my back.
Thank you for making me.   Amen.

VIVIANNA, 7

134

Our study of stained-glass windows took us to the cathedral in November. No sooner were we back at school than pictures of bright leaded panes began to take shape. Raymond's beautiful painting of a crucifixion window was matched by his excellent description.

Stained Glass Window

The stained-glass window glows
with golden colours, blue colours—
especially Our Lord on the cross
with golden halo bright.
Orange colours and many others too,
make a stained glass window.

RAYMOND, 7

The Stained-Glass Windows

The stained-glass window has all different colours. Bright colours are best for a church, with the beautiful picture of saints. Red and orange are the brightest colours. My picture is of Mary and Joseph with Jesus.

MICHAEL LE., 7

Stained-Glass Windows

Stained-glass windows
Big and strong
with holy pictures
all the way along.
All stained windows colourful
all the way along.

WADE, 7

The Assumption

Virgin Queen went up high
into the light of heaven.
Clouds covered her head.
Small angels stood at her feet.
God's happy face filled heaven
for Virgin would be crowned.

RAYMOND, 7

Walking in the garden one November evening I picked some tiny opening leaves of Liquid Amber. Each fine stem like a frail arm supported five stretching 'fingers'. I showed them to the children next day without drawing any comparisons. Carmella thought the leaves looked like someone's head. The rest saw them as hands.

The Leaves

Sister showed us some leaves. When the little leaves open up they are like hands praying to God.

LESLIE, 7

135

Baby Leaf

Baby leaf, baby leaf,
praying to God,
he too wants to be big and green
like the other leaves.

WADE, 7

New Leaf

It smells like perfume.
It looks like praying hands
and it opens out
to love God.
That's a new leaf.

CATHERINE, 7

Leaves

Open wide
praise to the Lord,
in your garden
lift up straight and tall.
He has given you everything.
Praise to the Lord our God.

THERESE, 7

Leaves

When little leaves need sun and rain
they open like little hands
praying to God.

ANTONY, 7

At recess time the other day I found myself making up a jingle:
'Have your milk, put your rods* away, tidy up and then go out to
play.' I saw Marianne chuckle to herself as she tidied her desk.
After play I found this note laughing up at me from my posting box.

Playtime

Have your milk. Have your play.
Then put your rods away.
Ha! ha! ha!
Time to have my milk.
Ho! ho! ho!
Time to have my play
Ting! ting! ting!
Time to put my rods away.

MARIANNE, 7

My posting box is often full of surprises. Sometimes all the
writing is on one very topical subject, at other times there is a
medley of themes.

* Coloured wooden rods used in the mathematics lessons.

Ice Cream

Smooth and yummy,
cold and scrummy,
creamy spoon.
(I am sure
someone had ice-cream today
and left a spoon
in our silver plate.)

RAYMOND, 7

Ducks

'Quack, quack', went the ducks
having a race
with all the other white ones.
They splash and paddle
with their feet.
They are eating their bread away.

MICHAEL LE., 7

Duck

The duck is peaceful . . .
He flaps his wings and splashes and the spray flies up
The water plops and he whirls around.
A secret he hears from the other ducks
and he flies to another spot.
He flies like a jet in the sky.
He skids like an outboard motor with his webbed feet.
He whacks his wings on the water . . .
Now he is calm.

PETER, 7

The Duck in the Pond

I will swim
and my feet will go
flappety, flappety, flap!
And when a person looks in the pool,
he will see all sorts of coloured ripples.

SILVANNA, 7

Duck

I am a duck.
I am all wet with showers.
Now I will fly in the sky.

MARTHES, 7

The Duck

You thrash,
you curve,
and land like a jet,
and stretch your wings
like any bird.

ANTON, 7

The Flight

This is a duck.
He is graceful when he swims across the lake.
He is quiet . . . He is dumb . . .
He moves slowly as he crosses the peaceful water.
He hears a secret message and starts to whirr his
wings.
He brings his body up and his feet out.
He spreads his wings and takes off to glide through
the air.
As he lands he stretches his feet and skids along the
water making a flying spray.

MICHAEL, 7

White Duck

White and pure
calm and sure
paddling in the water,
I see him diving
by my eyes.
He's got a fish.
Paddling under the bridge
is my pure white duck.

RAYMOND, 7

The Show

There are many wonderful things to see at the show. There are sheep,
horses, cattle and pigs. There are goats, cats, dogs, birds, also flowers,
cakes, jams and pieces that have been knitted by people. You can have
rides on ponies, buy fairy floss, dolls on sticks, or winky dolls. You can
watch the trotting races too.

KIM, 7

Rain

'Run quickly,
here comes the rain.
Run, run quickly.
You made it.
Now it is going
"Pitter-patter"
as it hits the ground.'

MARK A., 8

Rain

'Pitter-patter' all day long.
'Bang-bang' on the roof.
'Pitter-patter' on the ground.
'Snip-snip' on my hand.

ANTONY, 7

Rain

Rain rain going 'pitter-patter'
Rain rain going 'splash'
Clouds going 'boom'
Seas going 'crash'
and all sorts of things I hear.

TIMOTHY, 7

Rain

Little fairy rain drops
fall upon my roof top,
sparkle on the leaves,
drop on fields of grey,
fall along the sparkling river.

RAYMOND, 7

The visit of Sister Catherine from Bundi in the Territory of New Guinea revived the children's interest in New Guinea. Our specimens of a paradise bird, a belum, a coconut broom, a native drum and some huge insects were all carefully inspected. Christina Rosetti's poem about the Bird of Paradise was studied with deep awareness and is reflected in the children's work.

Paradise Bird

High up there
I see a bird
golden flame of wing.
King of birds
he flies high.
His name is unknown
through many lands.
It is the heaven bird I see,
the bird of paradise.

RAYMOND, 7

Paradise Bird

Silver and gold
and fine feathers
make a beautiful bird.
What kind of bird?
A paradise bird.
He makes a wheel
around my head.
It's like a golden fire
just started.

THERESE, 7

Paradise Birds

There are birds you do not know.
Birds with gold wings and silvery wings.
Some have green like moss,
and darting flames like red.
They are birds you have never seen,
the birds of paradise.

MICHAEL LO., 7

Birds of Paradise

Gold-winged and silver-winged
birds of paradise.
They fly and glide
through the air.
They mean a fortune
to a person
getting married in New Guinea.

TIMOTHY, 7

Paradise Bird

High in the sky
a bird was flying.
A bird with fiery wings.
Its wings shone
and it moved like a moving sun.
Up and down it went.

CATHERINE, 7

Drum

'Boom! Boom!' goes the Bundi drum
as they play it.
'Thud! Thud!' goes the drum.
It sounds like a giant footstep
coming close to you.

MARK A., 8

A Bundi Drum

Boom! Boom! we have a Bundi drum.
We play on it hard all day.
Night is here and we will sleep
but anything will wake us up.

ANTONY, 7

New Guinea Drum

Hollow big and strong,
dance high in the air.
Thunder thunder in the air.
—What's that?
Natives drumming.
Feathers high.
Masks they wear.
Fire! Fire!
Dance around!
Bang! Bang!
All around.

RAYMOND, 7

Drum

Drums drums heavy and hollow
'Boom! Boom!' they go.
Lizard skin heavy and thick
stretches across the top.
Natives dancing around the fire
strike, strike, strike, with their hands,
thudding the drum all the time,
booming and thudding
like a thunderbolt.

MICHAEL LE., 8

The Drums

'Thud! thud!' go the drums.
Natives are dancing.
Little Bundi hands
Big Bundi hands
banging on the drum.
Booming booming
Bang! Bang!
They all dance
round the fire.
Yah! Yah!
Boom! Boom!

KIM, 7

December comes hand in hand with Advent—and with it the
Advent Wreath Ceremony and the longing for the coming of the

Saviour. Christmas carols are practised for the carol festival and cribs are made for every home. Children's writing reflects the liturgical season:

Advent Wreath

Dear Jesus You are coming.
You are the Light of the World.
We will put up our Advent Wreath.
It will remind us of You.
We put four candles in it.
We light a candle each week.
When all the candles are lit
It is Christmas Day.

CATHERINE, 7

Advent Wreath

Advent means coming. There are only four weeks until Our Lord comes to us. I light a candle each week. I pray until the four weeks are finished and I sing quietly, too. The Light of the World is coming soon.

KIM, 7

Advent Wreath

Four weeks are in the four candles. When the four weeks are past, the Light of the World will come to us and we will praise the Lord for His great glory.

MICHAEL L., 7

Advent Wreath

Lord, I will light your candle each week. My last candle will be purple. On Christmas day I will change my candle into white.

ANTONY, 8

Advent Wreath

The Lord is coming, four weeks of prayer.
Light four candles one by one.
The Lord is coming, four weeks of prayer.

WADE, 8

The Advent Wreath

The Advent Wreath means
the coming of Our Lord.
Every week is one candle.
When all four candles are lit
that means Christmas is here.

TIMOTHY, 7

Advent

One week more
and we will sing
and the Lord will be here.
He will not appear.
But I'm sure He will be here.

MARIANNE, 7

Advent

Lord, it is nearly time for You to come.
The Advent Wreath is lighting, and
we will sing around it softly
to greet the coming of Christ.

MARIANNE, 7

A Christmas Carol

Sleep, sleep
Little King.
Sleep all night
wrapped in white linen,
lying in a manger.
Sleep all night.

KIM, 7

Carol

Sleep, sleep
quietly, hush.
In the manger's hay
a baby is born.
Softly and quietly He lay
and He was born on Christmas day.

CATHERINE, 7

Little Christ's Carol

Little King in a manger
born on hay
asleep He lay.
He is your King
the great one.
Kings from distant lands
gifts they bring
for the Christ Child
born in a manger.
Asleep He lay.
Eyes watched to see
the Christ Child
born on Christmas day.

RAYMOND, 7

143

Christmas Carol

Hush, rock, baby is asleep.
No time to weep.
It's Christmas.
Someone is born.
It's Jesus,
and Jesus is asleep.

MARIANNE, 7

Finally comes Michael L's last writing for this year. It is a gentle and serenely beautiful carol for a child of seven.

Carol

Sleep quietly
upon the hay
lovely little Jesus
born on Christmas day.
Mary looking
smiling at His face
eyes shining
hair silky
and full of grace.

We have reached the end of our year and for the first time my posting box is empty. Children's voices echo back to me as they go on their way for the Christmas holidays.

I sit at my desk and muse. Since we started with Words in Colour how changed our school days have been. It is true that I would be the last to coerce a teacher to use it because its acceptance implies a personal philosophy of teaching that amounts, for most of us, to a conversion. Yet all around me I see teachers who, having once taken the step, would not exchange their new and vital days for the old.

The loudest champion for Words in Colour is its success, for the fact of the transformation in the children cannot be denied. This is seconded by the clamour of the children themselves, as they continually ask for more.

I wish to thank these little children for sharing with me the treasures of their minds and thus helping me to write this book. I pray that they may, on account of our partnership, go forth more ready to meet the challenges that life will bring, and more fully equipped to use the powers of their minds and their own refreshing creativity.